D0853734

Sacrificed at the Alamo
Tragedy and Triumph in the Texas Revolution

MILITARY HISTORY OF TEXAS SERIES: NUMBER THREE

The Military History of Texas Series tells the colorful, dynamic, and heroic stories of the state's soldiers, battles, and battlefields from Spanish times to the present. The series promotes our mission to encourage traditional narratives and make history accessible to the broadest audience possible.

> Donald S. Frazier
> General Editor

The Military History of Texas Series, a project of the McWhiney Foundation in Abilene, is funded in part by grants from the Carl B. and Florence E. King Foundation and the Summerfield G. Roberts Foundation.

ALSO IN THE MILITARY HISTORY OF TEXAS SERIES:

The Finishing Stroke: Texans in the 1864 Tennessee Campaign
    by John R. Lundberg

The Wings of Change:
The Army Air Force Experience in Texas During World War II
    by Thomas E. Alexander

Sacrificed at the Alamo
Tragedy and Triumph in the Texas Revolution

Richard Bruce Winders

State House Press

McMurry University
Abilene, Texas

Library of Congress Cataloging-in-Publication Data

Winders, Richard Bruce, 1953-
      Sacrificed at the Alamo : tragedy and triumph in the Texas
      Revolution / Richard Bruce Winders.
          p. cm. -- (Military history of Texas series ; no. 3)
      Includes bibliographical references and index.
      ISBN 1-880510-80-4 (cloth : alk. paper) —
      ISBN 1-880510-81-2 (pbk. : alk. paper)

      1. Alamo (San Antonio, Tex.)--Siege, 1836.
2. Texas—History—Revolution, 1835-1836. I. Title. II. Series.
      F390 .W775 2004
      976.4'03--dc22

                                          2003026227

State House Press
McMurry Station, Box 637
Abilene, TX 79697-0637
(325) 793-4682

Printed in the United States of America

ISBN 1-880510-80-4
1-880510-81-2 (paper)

Book designed by Rosenbohm Graphic Design

Sacrificed at the Alamo is underwritten in part by a grant from the AVJ Foundation of Albany, Texas.

CONTENTS

MAPS AND ILLUSTRATIONS

CREDITS

The cover painting by Gary Zaboly is from the collection of Charlie Wilson. The schematic drawing of the Alamo and the illustrations of the Texians and the Mexicans are by Gary Zaboly and are published with permission from the Alamo. Maps are by Donald S. Frazier, Ph.D., Abilene, Texas.

INTRODUCTION

Some historical events capture the public's imagination more than others. Few would dispute that the battle of the Alamo is an event that has a strong hold on people worldwide. Even 168 years after the fall of the old mission, books and movies are still being written to tell the story. If past interest in the Alamo is any indication, the fascination with the famous battle is in no danger of diminishing.

Much of the modern discussion about the Alamo has been concerned with attempts to fill in details about the thirteen-day-long siege and battle. Alamo aficionados have a burning desire to learn all they can about the epic struggle. How many defenders were actually inside the fort? How many messengers did Travis send out with pleas for help? How many Hispanic defenders died fighting against their countryman, Antonio López de Santa Anna? Attention has been particularly focused on David Crockett, the best known member of the Béxar garrison. Did he actually wear a coonskin cap? More importantly, how did he die: fighting like a tiger or executed after the battle? The focus of these examinations might be described as micro-history because they look for answers to small historical questions. None of the answers will ultimately change the outcome of the battle. Moreover, some of the questions may be inherently unanswerable, sending researchers into an endless maze for which there is no exit. Still, people want to know and they will continue to look.

Sacrificed at the Alamo takes a different approach to the Alamo. My examination is on a broader scale and might be called macro-history. I want to establish a context for Alamo aficionados and scholars.

It is my contention that students of the battle will gain a greater appreciation of the event if they understand why it occurred. I suggest that it is more important in the long run to know the reason Crockett died rather than the exact manner of his death. This work presents a cohesive military and political analysis for the battle that is lacking from most previous studies. It still leaves plenty of room for the smaller questions but hopefully places the battle firmly in the larger historical picture.

Here are some ongoing movements in the 1830s of which the reader should be aware. The rise of republicanism threatened traditional governments and its adherents. The rise of the common man challenged old elites as the widening democratic circle gave more men a voice in political decisions. Citizen-soldiers battled the regular army for control of the military establishment, claiming that amateurs, too, knew how to win battles as proven by George Washington, William H. Harrison, and Andrew Jackson. These movements affected events both in the United States and Mexico and where the two nations intersected—Texas.

A word about terms used in this work will be useful. "American" refers to a person born in the United States of America. "Mexican" refers to a person born in Mexico, including native-born Texans. "Tejano" also refers to native-born Texans. "Republican" refers to the republican ideal or to its proponent. "Federalism" describes a system of government in which the states exist in an arrangement with a general or national government; "Federalist" refers to an adherent of Federalism. "Centralism" is a system of government in which power is concentrated in a general or national government at the expense of state sovereignty. "Béxar" is an older term for San Antonio. The men who ultimately died at the Alamo belonged to the "Béxar garrison" that included both the town and the old mission. Knowing how these terms are used in this study will prevent confusion.

A brief word about citations. Notes are used to (1) steer readers to standard works on various topics where they can find more information and (2) to document the sources of quotes and other specific information. In the latter case, a citation usually appears directly after the quotation. In some instances, however, a document may be the source for several paragraphs, in which case the citation appears after the last instance of its use.

Acknowledgments are certainly due. These include but are not limited to William Chemerka, James E. Crisp, William C. Davis, J.R. Edmondson, Bill Groneman, Stephen L. Hardin, Alan C. Huffines, Paul A. Hutton, Jack Jackson, Paul D. Lack, and Thomas Ricks Lindley. The work of these writers provides anyone studying the Alamo a solid foundation on which to build. A special tip of the hat goes to Kevin R. Young, someone to whom we all are indebted for his in-depth knowledge of the Alamo and his willingness to share it. My appreciation for comments on early versions of the manuscript go to Glenn Dromgoole, Don Frazier, Robert Pace, and Robert Wettemann. Thanks, too, go to the Daughters of the Republic of Texas who have allowed me to pursue my research and writing as Historian and Curator at the Alamo. The members of the Alamo's Education Department also deserve my thanks for providing me feedback as my interpretation evolved.

Chapter One
BACKGROUND OF
THE REVOLUTION

*They [the American colonists] all go about with their constitution in
their pocket, demanding their rights.*[1]
General Manuel Mier y Terán
1828 Inspection of Texas

Tired and worried, William B. Travis lay down on his bed inside his
Alamo headquarters to gain a few hours rest. Foremost on his
mind was the unanswered question of when the reinforcements
promised by the provisional government would arrive. His friend,
Robert M. Williamson, had said volunteers were on their way and
encouraged him to hold out a little longer. Twelve days had passed
since General Antonio López de Santa Anna began his siege. So far
the Béxar garrison had kept them at bay. The encirclement was complete, however, and the government troops could storm the old mission compound at anytime. Although not built as a fort, the Alamo
had been fortified. Would the garrison be able to hold off an attack
if it occurred before help arrived? Which would come first, salvation
or defeat?

Several hundred yards away Santa Anna already knew the answer.
His troops were moving into position to carry out a classic *coup de
main* or surprise attack against the makeshift fortress. The assault

would begin before sunrise so as to cloak his soldiers in darkness. If all went well, his columns would be at the walls before the garrison realized what was happening. Once driven from their defenses, the rebels would be rooted out and killed. How could a collection of farmers and adventurers stand against his experienced army? The approaching victory would rid Béxar of the troublesome foreigners and bring glory to him and his Centralist government. For the man who came to be called "The Napoleon of the West," recapturing the Alamo would be a small affair in the larger task of returning Texas to Mexican control.

THE RISE OF MODERN REPUBLICANISM

The Texas Revolution is best understood as an episode that occurred within the context of a larger ongoing Mexican civil war. To view it any other way is to isolate it from the people and events that produced it and shaped its course. The traditional story of the Battle of the Alamo, in which all of importance happened within the walls of the old mission, must be expanded beyond the boundaries of Texas to realize why the battle occurred at all.

Revolution swept the world as the nineteenth century dawned. The first outbreak had occurred in North America where thirteen of Great Britain's colonies had chosen to declare independence. The revolt next spread to France, carried there by soldiers returning from North America after having helped the former British colonies sever their ties with King George III and establish a new nation called the United States of America. France soon found itself in a life and death struggle against the rest of Europe when the French abolished their monarchy and set up a republican government. Republican movements spread throughout the world, back across the Atlantic to Spain's American colonies, and proved to be extremely virulent, still influencing world politics today.

The revolution grew out of the period of history known as the Enlightenment, a period in which philosophers debated the nature of man. A major concern for them was to discover the proper relationship between man and his government. It was obvious to most of these thinkers that society could not exist with man free to pursue his desires unhampered. The result of allowing such a system would be chaos and tyranny as the strong would always force their will on the weak. Laws were needed to check man's baser instincts in order to create an orderly society or civilization. The question was, however, from where should these laws come.

Prior to the Enlightenment, the world's nations had been ruled by monarchs. European kings and queens based their authority on religion, claiming that they had been chosen by God to protect His faith. The relationship between the monarch and his people was hierarchical; the people were subjects of the monarch and obligated to serve him. Little recourse existed in such a system supposedly ordained by God. Who had the right to question God's representative on earth?

The Enlightenment, coupled with the reforms of the Protestant Reformation, marked a shift in thinking by extending God's favor to all men. The change mirrored a shift in religious thought that stated that man had free will or the ability to choose how to worship God. All men could choose to have a close relationship with God, a notion that placed them on the same spiritual level with their monarch. Once this idea became generally accepted, the chain that bound a monarch and his subjects was broken. Rights were not the gift of the king but bestowed on all men by their Creator. If one accepted as fact that all men had been created equally, then all men were equally suited to make the laws that govern society. This simple shift in logic formed the basis of modern republican government.

As in the case of the United States, other former European colonies that had broken away from their homelands gained the opportunity to establish a new government to replace the hierarchical system if they chose to do so. Simon Bolivar, José de San Martín, and Bernardo O'Higgins made names for themselves as South American liberators. The opportunity for Mexico to challenge Spain came in 1821.[2]

Mexico was first rocked by revolution in 1810. Mexican intellectuals, including members of the lesser clergy, had absorbed many ideas of the Enlightenment. Native-born Spaniards, called *criollos*, faced discrimination at the hands of *gachupines* or Spaniards born in Spain who resided in Mexico. The royal patronage system awarded the most prized government, ecclesiastic, and military offices to *gachupines*. The denial of opportunity frustrated and angered *criollos*, who desired upward mobility. Many quietly discussed revolution as a way to remedy the situation, citing the examples of other recent revolts as their models for success.[3]

Events in Europe accelerated the revolutionary climate in Mexico. France had passed quickly through its republican phase and created the French empire of Napoleon Bonaparte. Napoleon had successfully defended France from the rest of Europe in the wars that resulted from the overthrow of the French monarchy. Having driven back his attackers, Napoleon invaded Spain in 1808, deposed King Ferdinand VII, and placed his brother, Joseph Bonaparte, on the Spanish throne. Napoleon's invasion disrupted communication between the Spanish colonies and their monarch.

Mexico's revolt erupted at the village of Dolores early on the morning of September 16, 1810. Its leader was Father Miguel Hidalgo y Costilla, the parish priest. He and his confederates incited the local villagers to rise against Spanish officials and other *gachupines* in the region. His followers were predominantly peasants who saw the war as a way to gain land and punish their Spanish oppressors. Hidalgo and his lieutenants found that they could not control the savage forces they had unleashed and were shocked to see the brutal acts of vengeance committed in the name of the revolution by their peasant army. Royalist forces made short work of Hidalgo, catching and executing him after first expelling him from the priesthood, but other rebels took to the mountains and jungles and began a guerrilla campaign against Spanish rule that would last for nearly ten years.

Napoleon's occupation of Spain allowed its colonies to experience a level of autonomy for the first time in their history. In Mexico, rebel leaders expanded their areas of control. Royalist officials had to contend with the rebellion without direction from Madrid. An event in Spain, however, would hold out the hope for home rule of an official nature that would eventually lead to independence.

Reacting to the invasion of their country, Spanish dissidents met at the city of Cadiz in 1812 and formed a new government based on a liberal constitution that would limit the authority of the king once he was returned to power. Delegates from the colonies were even invited to join the new congress, something that had been unheard of in the colonial system. The eventual defeat and withdrawal of the French allowed Ferdinand to return to the Spanish throne. Raised in the tradition of powerful monarchs, he refused to accept the Constitution of 1812 and set about ruling as he had before his French-provoked exile. In 1820, a group of army officers led by Colonel Rafael Riego threatened to oust Ferdinand unless he adopted the liberal ideas expressed in the constitution. Thus, even though still a monarchy, Spain had been forced to incorporate Enlightenment notions into its government.

The Riego Revolt shook Mexico. One of the features of Hidalgo's revolt that had been most upsetting was the attack on property and property holders. How would New Spain fare under a liberal Spanish government? Would peasants take it as a sign to renew their rampage? Could something be done to shield Mexican society from radical change? Separation from Spain might prevent the spread of radical reform to Mexico. The time for independence had arrived.

INDEPENDENCE AND THE FEDERAL REPUBLIC OF MEXICO

Independence from Spain offered Mexico a way to maintain public order and preserve the social status quo. Thus, Mexico's revolt was conservative in nature. Separation from Spain was accomplished when *criollo* army officers and insurgent leaders realized that their own interest lay in cooperating with each other to drive the royalists from Mexico. Colonel Agustín de Iturbide issued a call for the former enemies to join forces to create a new nation in which they—not the *gachupines*—controlled the government. Removing Spaniards from the system would allow *criollos* like Iturbide and the mestizos guerrillas he had been fighting to share real power. He crafted a program to establish an independent Mexico called the Plan of the Iguala or the Three Guarantees. The plan declared independence from Spain, kept Catholicism as the national religion, and promised equality among all Mexicans regardless of their caste. It also proposed to preserve the authority of the monarchy by inviting a European nobleman to come to Mexico and assume the Mexican crown. Iturbide's solution initially worked and the days of Spain's rule came to a close.[4]

Instead of becoming the nation's savior, Iturbide initiated a series of revolts and counter-revolts that wracked Mexico for decades. When no European nobleman came forward to accept the Mexican throne, Iturbide proposed that he become emperor and used his troops to support his bid for power. Thus, Mexico entered a brief imperial period as Iturbide assumed the title of Agustín I. His reign alienated many of Mexico's elite and middle class, who banded together to force his ouster and exile. Nevertheless, Iturbide had set an important precedent: the force of arms was an effective method to change government.

The imperial interlude allowed Mexicans who wanted to establish a federal republic an opportunity to advance their agenda. Wishing to abandon the centralized system they had experienced for years under Spain (and more recently Agustín I), delegates assembled to form a new government for Mexico and chose to establish a republic, somewhat modeled after the United States. Mexico would be divided into eighteen states and four territories that would cooperate through a national congress located in Mexico City. A plan of government, called the Federal Constitution of 1824, was adopted to define the powers of the various states and set forth their relationship to the national government and each other. A president, elected by the national congress, would serve as chief executive of the Federal Republic of Mexico. Each state was free to adopt its own constitution as long as it did not conflict with the federal document.[5]

Events in Mexico were relatively uneventful during the administration of its first president, Guadalupe Victoria. Unfortunately, the military stepped in during the next election (1828) to overturn the results. Victoria's legitimate successor, Manuel Gómez Pedraza, was forced into exile by former rebel general Vicente Guerrero, who assumed the presidency. Guerrero was subsequently overthrown by his own vice president, General Anastasio Bustamante. More conservative than Guerrero, Bustamente had the backing of Mexico's powerful trio: the Church, the landowners, and the army. These bodies were naturally fearful of de-centralization inherent in a true federal system because it threatened their traditional authority. Though staggered, Mexican federalism had not been dealt a deathblow . . . yet.

In 1832, General Antonio López de Santa Anna led a Federalist counter-revolt against Bustamante that restored Pedraza to the presidency. Santa Anna became Pedraza's successor and a hero to the Federalists for restoring the federalist system. Santa Anna soon withdrew to his estate near Vera Cruz and turned the actual administration of the government over to his vice president, Valentín Gómez Farías.

Gómez Farías belonged to a small group of radical federalists who wanted to restructure Mexican society. He threatened Mexico's elites (church, landowners, and army) by promoting legislation that if enforced would confiscate Church property, redistribute land, and reduce the size of the army. Faced with the very real challenge posed by the vice president and his supporters in the national congress, representatives from these bodies approached Santa Anna and in effect asked him to lead a Centralist counter-revolution against his own administration. Never one burdened by principle except that of retaining power, Santa Anna accepted the offer, marched to Mexico City, dismissed Gómez Farías, disbanded the national congress, and replaced it with Centralist supporters. Acting under the Plan of Cuernavaca, the new regime announced that the Federal Constitution of 1824 would be replaced with a new one that reflected the centralization of power that was about to take place. Mexico's experiment with the federal system of government had come to an end.[6]

TEXAS AND ITS PEOPLE

Texas has always been a borderland to the Europeans who came to the region. Borderlands are potentially places of conflict by their very nature. On the international front, Texas early on came to represent the contest between Spain and France to establish a colonial empire in the American southwest.[7]

The Spaniards had been building a colonial empire in Mesoamerica since Hernando Cortés began his conquest of the Aztecs in 1519. The center of New Spain lay at Mexico City, the former Aztec capital. Expeditions had worked outward from Mexico City to overcome the more barbaric native people and develop the newly conquered regions economically. Texas, at the northern end of New Spain, lay outside of Spain's central focus and posed little interest until an international rival encroached on this far-flung Spanish land.

The rival was France, who attempted to establish Fort St. Louis on Matagorda Bay in 1685. Illness and Indians ended the effort and Robert Cavelier's (better known as La Salle) settlement vanished from the landscape. The French incursion into Texas, however, convinced Spanish officials that something must be done to strengthen their king's claim to the region. The best way to accomplish this was by establishing a human presence in Texas.

Spain had been conquering frontiers for years with the twin institutions of the mission and presidio. Missionaries worked to convert the native population into useful Spanish subjects. Soldiers, stationed at nearby *presidios*, protected the missionaries from hostile Indians and served as truant officers for neophytes who tried to return to their previous lifestyle. The system worked by offering incentives to bring and keep converts at the mission voluntarily and force (or the threat of it) to hold the converts in place. Missions and presidios sprang up in Texas throughout the eighteenth century. When the Spain gained control of Louisiana prior to France's defeat in the French and Indian War, the international threat to Texas passed along with the need for the missions and presidios.

The arrival of the Spaniards in Texas initiated a dynamic period in which different groups of people intermixed, forming the basis for a new culture. The indigenous tribes generally fell into a category called Coahuilatecans, meaning people who lived in the region of Coahuila and Texas. These formed the bulk of the mission Indians. The Spanish missionaries and soldiers were accompanied by Tlaxcalans, members of a band allied to the king since the time of Cortés. Intermarriage between the Spaniards, Tlaxcalans, and

Coahuilatecans produced a regional population called *Tejanos* (Spanish for a person from Texas).

Other people eventually came to Texas. In 1731, a group of families from the Canary Islands settled in the town of San Antonio de Béxar, augmenting the population that, until then, had consisted of soldiers, missionaries, and converts. The real change in Texas's population, however, would not come until large numbers of Anglo-Americans flowed into the region late 1820s. The period of American immigration would not take place until after the creation of an independent Mexico, though.

Not all of Texas's native population had welcomed the missionaries and soldiers. Nomadic raiders such as the Comanche had little use for the small Spanish communities that had sprung up in Texas other than as places that could supply livestock and human captives. Mission residents and presidio garrisons had to keep alert against mounted war parties that swept down on the isolated compounds without warning. The vast distance of the region from Mexico's population centers, combined with the almost constant threat posed by these raiders, thwarted Spanish officials' attempts to entice settlers to the Texas frontier.

Unable to populate the frontier with their own people, Spain turned to another source: Americans. Moses Austin approached officials in San Antonio de Béxar in 1819 and offered to bring settlers to Texas. He had lived in Missouri at the time when it was under Spanish control. Officials believed that he and other former Spanish subjects would help develop the region if allowed to relocate to the Texas frontier. Immigrants were expected to become loyal Spanish subjects, with all that entailed, in exchange for permission to enter the king's territory.

The Spaniards never had the opportunity to carry out their colonization plan before Mexico declared its independence. Colonization was not dead, however, as Iturbide adopted the plan for his empire. The need for a stable population in Texas was so great that the plan continued in effect even after Iturbide had been deposed and the federal republic had been created. Moses Austin, too, never had the opportunity to colonize Texas, but others, including his son, Stephen F. Austin, did.

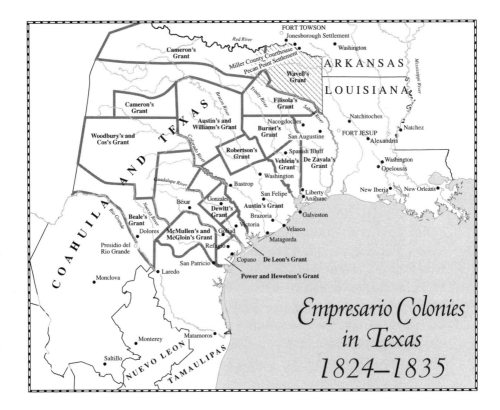

Mexico, although it favored immigration, wanted to control the flow of Americans and Europeans into Texas. A system was created through which land agents, designated *empresarios*, would accept responsibility for recruiting respectable men and women as colonists. In return for land, colonists had to agree to become law-abiding Mexican citizens, including conversion to Catholicism. For his trouble, the *empresario* was allowed to collect a twelve-and-a-half cent per acre administrative fee from each colonist to whom he assigned land. Tax exemptions were also granted colonists, giving them time to establish their homesteads before being asked to contribute to the nation's treasury. Thus, in return for making its public land available for settlement, the Republic of Mexico hoped to turn the Texas frontier into a productive and civilized region.

In 1828 the Mexican government sent General Manuel de Mier y Terán to Texas to assess the situation in Texas created by opening the region to mainly American colonists. He reported that the system had worked all too well. In fact, in the area of the American settlements, American-Mexicans outnumbered native-born Mexicans by ten to one. The Mexican government quickly realized that it had an immigration problem and only swift action could save Texas from being lost.

The government's response to the "Americanization" of Texas was the passage of the Law of April 6, 1830. It left immigration open to Europeans but decreed that immigrants could no longer come from countries that shared a border with Mexico, which meant the United States. Furthermore, the law included other measures designed to reassert the government's control over Texas and its citizens. The tax exemptions that were due to end would not be renewed when they expired. Tax officers would be sent to Texas to establish customs houses. The rule that prevented Anglo settlements from being built on the coast was reiterated. New forts were slated to be constructed throughout Texas to enforce these new regulations as well as maintain a strong government presence.

Reaction from the Americans was mixed. Many American-Mexicans believed that the government was within its rights to enact these measures, even if they did not agree with them. These were mostly people who had entered Texas through the *empresario* system and were therefore legal immigrants. Others, who had entered Texas on their own without the government's knowledge, had little respect for Mexico's sovereignty. The seeds of revolt had been planted as gradually more Americans (both legal and illegal) began to complain about the Mexican government's intrusion into their lives. But it was the rise of the Centralists and the revocation of the Federal Constitution of 1824 that brought the revolution to a head.

It is a mistake, however, to view the revolt simply as an uprising by American colonists against the Mexican government. The context for the revolt is a larger civil war that was occurring in Mexico. Native-born Mexicans living in Texas (Tejanos) were also ready to revolt against the government headed by General Santa Anna. Many

24

Tejanos had formed community and economic ties with the incoming Americans. Moreover, Tejanos looked to the United States, especially New Orleans, for trade. Tejanos were also in tune with the American views on the nature of a federal republic and felt disconnected from the national government in Mexico City. Thus, Tejano discontent contributed to the revolt brought on by the Centralists' dismantling of Mexico's federal republic.[8]

The growing resentment against the Centralists would ultimately erupt in revolt. No insurgent movement, however, could be sustained without an army. Texas's attempt to build a reliable military force is an integral part of the story of the Alamo. An examination of military trends of the period reveals much about the men who became caught up in the revolutionary events of 1835-1836.

Chapter Two
The Art of War in 19th Century North America

"... the men only went out to fight and return to their homes in ten days; they have been out for months, and many of them half clad, having taken only one suit of clothing."[1]
Major General Sam Houston
November 30, 1835

The members of the Alamo's garrison well knew that night was not a time to let down their guard. Military doctrine and common sense both dictated that darkness gave attackers an advantage. Unseen, the enemy could approach a sleeping force without resistance. And the garrison did want to sleep. Twelve days under constant siege had been fatiguing and wore on their nerves. All the more reason to be vigilant. Pickets manned posts outside the walls, ready to give the alarm if needed.

Centralist soldiers had carefully been moved into positions around the old mission. Their officers had given specific orders: "Don't talk." "Don't smoke." "Don't make any noise at all." Lying on the cold ground, they could see the occasional silhouette of a rebel who mounted the wall. Perhaps they could hear the pickets talking low among themselves as they sat peering out into the darkness.

Time seemed to stand still. It seemed a shame to have to spend what might well be one's last hours on earth cold, damp, and unable to move, but surprise must be maintained at all costs. The lives of comrades were at stake. The stillness gave the *soldados* as well as the Béxar garrison a chance to reflect on the events that had brought them to this point.

FOLLOWING THE EUROPEAN TRADITION

The armies of the Texas Revolution did not spring entirely from whole cloth. Both Americans and Mexicans organized their respective military establishments along European lines. After all, both had begun their existence as subjects of European nations. Furthermore, the early successes of Napoleon Bonaparte reinforced the notion of European superiority in martial matters. French success on the Continent, at least until Waterloo, gave the world a model of military efficiency worthy of emulation and in theory provided the context for the campaigns of the Texas Revolution.[2]

The man from Corsica infused life into what had become a predictable tactical system. Napoleon's Grande Armée best epitomized the two tactical formations that had evolved through the centuries of European warfare: the line and the column. These two elements existed prior to Napoleon's appearance; he, however, added a third—maneuverability. Students of the general, both in the United States and Mexico, were aware of his principles, even though adherents to his doctrines did not always possess his level of mastery.

The line had developed originally as a way for a commander to maximize his firepower. In its simplest form, a line-of-battle consisted of multiple ranks of soldiers who were placed shoulder to shoulder and facing the enemy. Geometrically, it was wider than it was deep. Units were arranged in three ranks during the early days of muskets. It was believed that a three-rank formation allowed the unit to deliver a rapid and sustained rate of fire by alternating the fire between each rank. The drawback of the three-rank system was that it presented a narrow front to the enemy. By the early nineteenth

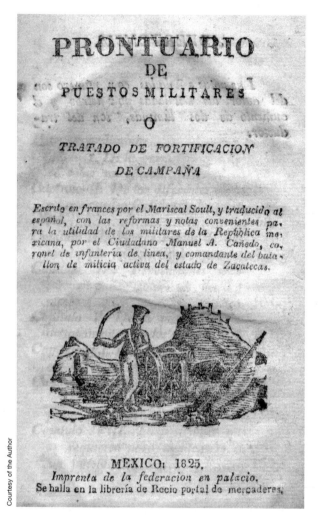

PRONTUARIO
DE
PUESTOS MILITARES
O
TRATADO DE FORTIFICACION
DE CAMPAÑA

Escrito en frances por el Mariscal Soult, y traducido al
español, con las reformas y notas convenientes pa-
ra la utilidad de los militares de la República me-
xicana, por el Ciudadano Manuel A. Cañedo, co-
ronel de infantería de línea, y comandante del bata-
llon de milicia activa del estado de Zacatecas.

MÉXICO: 1825.
Imprenta de la federación en palacio.
Se halla en la librería de Recio portal de mercaderes.

*This 1825 publication shows that the Mexican military
trained in Napoleonic tactics.*

century, most armies had come to utilize two ranks instead of three. Two ranks, which covered a wider front with the same amount of men, could still alternate their fire between ranks when required. Both the American and Mexican militaries commonly deployed their troops in a two-rank line-of-battle prior to and during the Texas Revolution.

On large battlefields, though, the line often had more depth than just a single line of units deployed facing the enemy. In this case, the line consisted of a series of units placed in succession. The benefit of this arrangement was that it created more mass, allowing an attack to be delivered in waves. It also meant that an attacker would have to break through successive lines in order to reach the enemy's rear. The limited number of troops used during the Texas Revolution, however, rarely permitted a commander to use successive lines-of-battle.

The column was the deepest of all tactical formations. It consisted of several units formed in a line-of-battle placed one behind the other. Geometrically, it was longer than it was wide. The narrow front presented by a column meant that its firepower was extremely limited. In battle, a column had the mass needed to punch through an enemy's line. Columns were also routinely used to move units from one location to another either while on the march or even during a battle.

For nineteenth century armies such as those of the Texas Revolution, lines and columns were made up of the following basic building blocks: companies, battalions, brigades, and divisions. In theory, the ideal strength of a company was approximately one hundred men, although this number was rarely reached or maintained. The commander of a company was a captain, assisted by various lieutenants, sergeants, and corporals. Eight companies (usually designated companies-of-the-line) were grouped to form a battalion. A battalion, also sometimes referred to as a regiment, was commanded by a colonel assisted by a lieutenant colonel, major, and an administrative staff. Two or more battalions could be united to form a brigade, commanded by a brigadier general assisted by a staff. Two or more brigades could be united to form a division, commanded by a major general and a staff. With subtle differences, this arrangement provided the framework for the insurgent and Centralist armies of the Texas Revolution.

Napoleon revolutionized warfare by insisting that his forces be maneuverable, both on and off the battlefield. Logistics of the day made it difficult to feed large numbers of men and livestock. The solution was for brigades and divisions to march several days apart from each other because the quartermaster and locals found it easier to supply smaller concentrations of troops. The danger an army faced when dispersed, though, was that isolated units could be attacked and defeated in detail before help could be summoned. Both the insurgents and Centralists encountered military reverses at various times in the revolution because their troops advanced beyond supporting distance of their comrades. Each side paid a high price for breaking this important military dictum.

Napoleon insisted on better communication and cooperation between his commanders so he could reassemble his army relatively quickly. He used forced marches, not only to reunite his scattered division, but also to appear when and where the enemy did not expect him, which gave him strategic control during his campaigns. Maneuver was also important on the battlefield. Napoleon's generals had trained their units to advance rapidly. Moreover, his troops could change quickly from line to column or column to line, something that gave him the ability to take advantages of any tactical weakness the enemy exhibited. The ability to maneuver against slower foes proved to be a substantial advantage for the French, something that their enemies learned by experience. The Centralist troops, because they were more experienced and came from a military establishment, were able to achieve speed and surprise on several occasions where the insurgents tended to be tied to static positions.

Armies at the time of the Texas Revolution still relied on the flintlock as their main small arm. The muskets could be loaded and fired three times a minute and had an effective range of around 100 yards. Fitted with an 18 inch bayonet, the musket was a formidable weapon at close range whether loaded or not. Some special units were beginning to be armed with a military version of

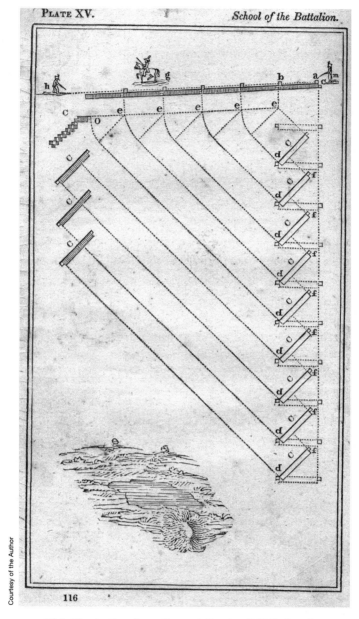

PLATE XV. School of the Battalion.

116

This illustration from Cooper's Tactics *(1836) showing a battalion changing from a column of companies to a line-of-battle.*

the rifle. The tight fit required by the ball for accuracy increased the time needed to load the weapon. The process could take a minute or longer when loading with loose powder, ball, and patch; using cartridges sped the process to two or three shots per minute but accuracy was lost because the ball did not form as tight a seal as when loaded more carefully. The effective range of the military rifle was about two hundred yards. Insurgent leaders routinely recommended that volunteers to their cause bring muskets with them to Texas.

North America had given rise to the use of civilian hunting rifles in warfare. In the hands of a marksman, the rifle could strike targets at three hundred yards. Loading, was slow, however, because a rifleman usually used loose powder, ball, and patch. The military had tried to incorporate range and accuracy of the hunting rifle by developing military rifles. The hunting rifle had drawbacks when used on campaign because they tended to be fragile and were not fitted with a bayonet for fighting at close quarters. Although some colonists and volunteers owned rifles, the use of such weapons in the revolution was less than popularly imagined. Both the United States Army and Mexican Army had military rifles as part of their arsenals, insuring that U.S. manufactured martial rifles and British imported Baker Rifles saw action in Texas.

The North American terrain was different from Europe, meaning that battlefields were different, too. Much of the countryside was still wooded, making if difficult for armies to pass through some areas in dense formations. Conversely, forested areas or tree-lined riverbanks offered riflemen protection and concealment from which they could put their weapons to the fullest use. The open prairie, however, favored more traditional massed formations, especially mounted troops when employed against men on foot. To be effective, commanders had to know how to use the terrain to their best advantage based on the capabilities of their troops. Napoleonic tactics, therefore, tended to be conducted on a small rather than grand scale but nevertheless they were evident on the battlefields of Texas.[3]

THE ARMY AND THE REPUBLIC

The rise of republican governments at the end of the eighteenth century changed the nature of the national armies. By tradition, armies had been raised by monarchs and owed their allegiance to the king or queen. Royal armies were paid from the king's treasury and commanded by officers loyal to him. There was a clear gulf between officers and enlisted men that mirrored monarchical society since the officers were nobles and enlisted men were commoners. Discipline was harsh and enlisted men rarely had the opportunity to become officers. A king's army could be augmented with mercenaries, foreign troops either offered for hire by another king or individuals who made their living as soldiers of fortune. It was a strict system intended to preserve the status quo that existed in a monarchical society.[4]

The traditional military model fell into disfavor in the new republics that emerged in the first quarter of the nineteenth century. Allegiance was now rendered to the nation, not its leader. Defense of one's country was viewed as a civic duty, giving rise to the notion that a nation's army should be made up of its citizens. As such, officers and enlisted men were drawn from the same social class (that made up of citizens), which supposedly eliminated the wide gulf that traditionally separated them. Passage from the ranks to the officer corps was expected and encouraged. Citizen-soldiers were organized by the various states; these states' armies were called the militia. However, planners believed that citizen-soldiers should not be called away from their employment unless in time of emergency. Reluctantly, they recognized the need for a regular army to guard the frontier and coast although its number was to be kept as small as possible. A republic needed no standing army that might turn against it. Thus, republican armies, in theory, were much different from armies of the past because they reflected a more open society.

Another difference existed between royal and republican armies. The officers and enlisted men of a monarch entered into a lifetime of service, retiring only when disabled or too aged to continue. Conversely, service in republican forces was intended to be temporary, terminating at the end of whatever emergency necessitated the militia's mobilization. Citizen-soldiers were expected to return to their fields, workbenches, and shops and pick up life where they had left off. A record of successful military service enhanced the chance of a former citizen-soldier if he chose to run as a candidate for an elected political office, a fact that fueled competition in war for rank and glory.

The notion of the citizen-soldier became extremely popular with republicans both in the United States and Mexico and state militias were organized throughout both countries. In Mexico, however, the national army was somewhat successful in resisting the establishment of a citizen-soldiery. The United States was another story as the citizen-soldier model dovetailed perfectly with the expansion of Jacksonian democracy, prompting a serious debate over the merits of volunteers vs. a regular army. Proponents of the regular army contended that a professional military force was needed to perform routine duties that citizen-soldiers would not. An army of professional officers and soldiers provided a trained cadre in case of a national emergency around which a volunteer army could be formed. Opponents of the regular army countered that the soldiers were mere "hirelings" who could not find gainful employment outside the army. Thus, it was un-American to have "hirelings," some of whom were not even citizens, as the defenders of the young republic.[5]

The regular army committed another serious breach of republican principle by the undemocratic manner officers increasingly were appointed to the service. Opponents argued that the government used the U.S. Military Academy to reward the wealthy by sending their sons to a free school on the Hudson River. Thus, West Point and its graduates became a lightning rod for supporters of the militia system. One of the most vocal critics of the Military Academy was Congressman David Crockett from Tennessee. In 1830, Crockett introduced a resolution stating "That said institution should be abolished, and the appropriations annually made for its support be discontinued." In addition to charging that the school gave the sons

of rich men an unfair advantage over those of the poor, he contended it was not needed in their current republican society. According
the record of congressional debates, Crockett remarked, "Another
bad effect of it was, that no man could get a commission in the army
unless he had been educated at West Point, but the army had been
headed very well by men who never went to that academy." He
recalled his own service in the Creek War, saying he had "gone out
and performed his twelve months tour of duty in the defence of his
country, as well as he could." So did "thousands of poor men who
had also gone out to fight their country's battles, but none of them
had [been] at West Point, and none of them had any sons at West
Point." His conclusion was that "A man could fight the battles of his
country, and lead his country's armies, without being educated at
West Point."[6] Many of Crockett's countrymen shared his low opinion of a regular army with a trained officer corps and carried this
bias with them to Texas. The question of which type of army was
right for Texas occupied the attention of the insurgents for some
months once the revolution erupted.

FRONTIER DEFENSE

Indian raids and other local emergencies required quick action
that could not wait for the mobilization of the established military
bureaucracy. Upon learning of the threat, members of the community gathered together to form an ad hoc expedition to defend, punish, or attack, depending on the needs of the specific situation.
These tended to be rather democratic units in which members of the
expedition frequently elected their commander as well as any other
officers needed. These expeditions had limited aims and, once met,
ended with everyone returning home to resume their civilian pur-
suits. Historian Thomas W. Cutrer has labeled this community
response the "frontier military tradition."[7] Although most likely seen
as an American phenomena, the residents of all frontiers commonly
respond in kind to emergencies. Anglo colonists carried the tradition
with them to Texas, but Tejanos were no strangers to it.

Soldiers of the Texas Army

The system had benefits. Reaction to the emergency could be quick because those responding to it were local. Those answering the emergency were highly motivated because they had a personal stake in retrieving stolen property, captive friends and relatives, or otherwise exerting justice for a wrong committed against their community. The expeditions were usually self-sufficient because each member provided his own mount, weapons, and food. Campaigns tended to be short because of the limited objective; moreover, its members could not be away from their homes and livelihoods for extended periods.

Despite its usefulness, the frontier military tradition had serious drawbacks. Some emergencies were greater than the local community's ability to handle. Additionally, these expeditions could not be kept in the field for an extended time because their members were needed at home and in their communities. Long term logistical support was difficult at best. Perhaps most important of all, the democratic nature of such ventures when conducted by Americans created an environment where the independent-minded volunteers could and would challenge their leaders' decisions, meaning that military discipline was almost non-existent. Although good men in a fight where personal courage and honor mattered, these volunteers had difficulty following orders.

Another frontier defense organization operated to provide ongoing protection—the ranging company. These units, which often had some official status, were made up of men who volunteered for this robust service. Ranging companies in North America dated back to the early days of the English colonies, as in the case of Rogers' Rangers that operated during the French and Indian War. However, the idea of ranging companies also existed in New Spain, where *companías volantes*, or flying companies, patrolled places like Texas. One such flying company, *La Compañía Volante de San Carlos de Parras*, used former Mission San Antonio de Valero—also known as the Alamo—as its home base. Its members battled Comanche raiders years before the establishment of the more famous Texas Rangers.

THE MILITARY ESTABLISHMENT AND THE TEXAS REVOLUTION

Mexico's federal government, which had only been formed in 1823, modeled its military on the old Spanish Royal Army. Native-born officers and soldiers, who were veterans of that service, formed a significant part of the new Mexican Army. The Plan of Iguala adopted in 1821 had supposedly mended the rift between former enemies by promising independence, equality, and the protection of the Catholic religion. An outward manifestation of this reunification was the inclusion of many former rebels, both officers and enlisted men, into the new national army. Another group was allowed into service: foreign-born officers. These included men who had been born in other Spanish dominions, European nations, and even the United States. Thus, the Mexican national army was a conglomerate of var-

Artwork by Gary Zaboly, Courtesy of the Alamo

Soldiers of the Centralist Army of Mexico

ious entities whose interests did not always coincide, a fact responsible for the army's interference in national politics. While in theory a republican army, it actually retained many of the traits characteristic of the royal army from which it sprang.[8]

The Mexican Army was composed partly of regular units called *permanentes* to reflect their permanent status. The Mexican military establishment consisted of ten regular infantry regiments at the time of the Texas Revolution. These had been reorganized in 1833 and given new designations that honored heroes from Mexico's independence movement: Hidalgo, Allende, Morelos, Guerrero, Aldama, Jiménez, Landero, Matamoros, Abasolo, and Galeana. A battalion of military engineers, or *Zapadores*, was also raised at that time. The Mexican Army had six regular regiments of mounted troops that had also survived the reorganization of 1833.[9] These were named for locations in which they were raised: Tampico, Dolores, Vera Cruz, Palmar, Iguala, and Cuatla. Although not all *permanentes* would be mobilized for the Texas campaign, the majority of Mexico's regular army would be sent to subdue the rebellious department. No medical department was officially organized until August 1836, months after the Texas Campaign had concluded.[10]

The *permanente* regiments were augmented by *activos* or militia units. Designated "active militia" because they had been called into service, some of these units had as much experience as their regular counterparts. The *activos* that participated in the Texas Campaign included battalions from San Luis Potosí, Toluca, Guadalajara, and Tres Villa.

The Mexican Army's artillery was not as well organized as the other branches of service. Its guns were a collection of old Spanish relics and new pieces that had recently been acquired in the move to update the national army. These pieces followed the older Gribeauval system in which artillery consisted of 4, 8, and 12 pound field guns, and 6 and 8 inch howitzers. Split trail carriages were still in use and mobility was limited. Guns and personnel were assigned to support the infantry as needed. The artillery was often paired with the *Zapadores* because of the similar nature of their roles.

The ranks were filled by both voluntary enlistment and by conscription. Men who volunteered served an eight-year enlistment; those who were forced to join served for ten years. Since most enlisted men, whether conscript or not, came from the same socio-economic class, the short enlistment was held out as an incentive to enter the service voluntarily. Convicts were sometimes used to fill out the army's ranks. Pay was low and regulated by the unit's commander. The government made no provision for soldiers' families so they often took them along on campaign in classic "camp follower" fashion. Called *soldaderas*, these noncombatants cooked and cared for their loved ones, relieving the military of some of the burdens associated with existing in the field.

The Mexican Army also relied on auxiliaries such as *presidial* troopers and local ranchers who operated somewhat along the lines of the frontier military tradition. These men knew the countryside and local inhabitants, something that made them valuable as scouts and spies. The intelligence they provided enabled the army to move through unfamiliar terrain and at times achieve surprise over the enemy.

Mexico had produced several military heroes in its short history through its barracks revolutions and invasion by Spain. Foremost among this group was Antonio López de Santa Anna, who had begun his career in the royalist army helping to put down uprisings in the wake of Father Hidalgo's 1810 revolt. He had been cited for bravery at the Battle of Medina, an 1813 engagement that took place near Béxar after American and Mexican republicans invaded Texas and established an independent republic. He supported the Plan of Iguala before turning against Iturbide. His switch characterized his lack of principle as he often picked one cause and then abandoned it for another. In 1829, Santa Anna was co-commander of an expedition to repel a Spanish army that had landed and occupied the port city of Tampico. For his victory, he earned the title of the "Hero of Tampico." Santa Anna won praise from Federalists throughout Mexico when he led a counter-revolt against the Centralists in 1832. His popularity insured for him the presidency of Mexico. Ironically, one of his former supporters, General José Antonio Mexía, rebelled against Santa Anna when the president embraced Centralism. Expelled from Mexico, Mexía traveled to New Orleans, where he plotted how to remove Santa Anna from power and restore federalism to his country.[11]

The American colonists also had a military hero whom they admired. Andrew Jackson had risen to national prominence due to his victories in the War of 1812. In 1814, Jackson commanded a successful assault against the Creek Indians at the Battle of Horseshoe Bend in the territory that would become the state of Alabama. He then went on to successfully defend the city of New Orleans from an assault by British regulars on January 8, 1815, a date that rivaled the Fourth of July in importance in the days of the early American republic. His victories offered mixed messages to his followers. At Horseshoe Bend, Jackson had led his fellow Tennessee militiamen to a stunning victory when they attacked and carried a fortified Indian village located in a bend of the Tallapoosa River. Thus, one could believe that citizen-soldiers could overcome great odds if resolute and well-led. Conversely, the Battle of New Orleans seemed to prove that citizen-soldiers could with the same determination and leadership hold their own against a veteran army fresh from the battlefields of Europe. Americans seemed to brush aside as unimportant the facts that Jackson, who had received a general's commission in the United States Army, had commanded regulars as well as volunteers at both battles or that his line at New Orleans had been strengthened considerably by artillery manned by Jean Lafitte's men. The lesson that Americans chose to learn was that the frontiersman armed with a long rifle would ultimately triumph over any foe in battle—Indian, British, and certainly Mexican.[12]

Many of the colonists who went to Texas had ties to Old Hickory, a sobriquet by which Jackson was known. One such man, Sam Houston, was destined to play a significant role in the Texas Revolution. A junior officer in the U.S. Army, Houston had participated in the assault at Horseshoe Bend. Grievously wounded, he nevertheless caught the attention of Jackson for his bravery. Houston, who was also from Tennessee, subsequently became a political protégé of the old war hero and future leader of the Democratic Party. The failure of the Creeks to hold their breastworks at Horseshoe Bend seemed to convince Houston that an army should not rely on fortifications, a philosophical view that is important to consider since he was to become the commander of the Texan military forces.[13]

Although the Centralists inherited Mexico's national army, the Texans were forced to raise their army virtually from scratch. They used the existing military model as their guide. Stephen F. Austin had created a militia for his colony in 1824 shortly after being granted a lieutenant colonel's commission by the Mexican government. He commanded a battalion of five companies made up of his colonists. He insisted on discipline and regularly held musters. Many colonists, not only those brought by Austin, had performed militia service in the United States. Although the militia proved unable to meet the demands of the revolution, this type of military service was not unknown to many men who eventually served against Santa Anna.

Texas was hard pressed to create a field army. The colonists who turned out at the beginning of hostilities exhibited all the characteristics associated with citizen-soldiers. Without a viable militia the colonists initially had to rely on ad hoc units of the type associated with the frontier military tradition in order to respond to emergencies as they occurred. By December 1835, the colonists found they had to rely on volunteers, many from the United States, to fill their ranks. Sam Houston's fledgling regular army failed due to lack of time and money. The story of Texas's attempt to build a military establishment is directly related to the Alamo and its fall.

Chapter Three
Texas in Revolt

We have sworn to support a federal republican govt., not a military usurpation—Republicanism not Centralism, which is but another word for Monarchy.[1]
William B. Travis

Inside the old mission, friends of Samuel Maverick and Jesse B. Badgett wondered if they had made it to the small town of Washington-on-the-Brazos. The garrison had elected the two men to represent them at the convention that was to have begun on March 1. Travis and his men fully expected independence would be declared. Although the revolt had begun in the name of the Federal Constitution of 1824, it had evolved into a demand for a separate nation, a republic model after the United States. These men had been suckled on the milk of freedom that only a republican government could provide. No doubt, though, these were free-born men who would not stand for any form of tyranny—real or imagined. Perhaps a rider might come in the morning with word independence had been declared. Perhaps reinforcements would bring the good news with them.

The issue of Federalism vs. Centralism may not have mattered to many of the *soldados* positioned around the Alamo, waiting for the signal to attack. They had seen revolts before, often being used as the very instruments to depose or install men who looked down upon them with disdain. Did their life improve with each change? Their

43

officers might benefit by the frequent political squabbles, but the spoils failed to trickle down. However, the revolt in Texas was different. Foreigners and disloyal Mexicans had dared to challenge Mexico over the ownership of this land. And had not the army been promised great rewards for reclaiming Texas? Federalism or Centralism? What did it matter if the projected military settlements in Texas proved opportunities for a fruitful life after the foreigners were gone.

Origins of the Conflict: Federalism Under Attack

The Centralist overthrow of the Federal Republic of Mexico, as directed in the Plan of Cuernavaca, stirred the Federalists into action. Although it was ultimately able to roll back the hated reforms, the Centralist government soon found itself forced to stamp out opposition to its concentration of power in Mexico City. The campaign to squelch Federalist dissent would eventually lead Santa Anna to Texas but not before he dealt with another rebellious state first.

Support for the Federalist Republic and its Constitution of 1824 tended to be strongest in the states most distant from Mexico City. Communication with the capital had always been slow due to the vast distances that had to be crossed. Isolation had caused the states that composed Mexico's borderlands to develop an attitude of independence and self-reliance. In such instances, local authority was believed to be best suited to deal with local problems. Thus, the idea of a centralized government imposing dictates from Mexico City did not sit well with many frontier inhabitants. The adoption of the Plan of Cuernavaca, which promised to dismantle the Constitution of 1824 and strip Mexico's states of their sovereignty and convert them into centrally controlled provinces, posed a real threat to independent-minded Texans—both Anglo and Tejano.

Several states voiced opposition to the new national government. The Centralists had to confront and overcome any resistance in order to secure their hold over the nation. The first state to be subdued was Zacatecas northwest of Mexico City. The conflict between Mexico City and Zacatecas was over the size of the state's militia. The

Centralists claimed that the various militias of the Mexican states had grown too large and were siphoning money from other much-needed projects. In order to reduce the number of these state armies, Centralist officials established the ratio of one militiaman for every five hundred people. Additionally, all private weapons not associated with military service were to be turned over to the national authorities. Although there may have been merit to the government's claim that the militias were too costly to be maintained at their current levels, the reductions of these armed bodies certainly lessened the chances of successful resistance to the wave of Centralism that was sweeping across Mexico.

Zacatecas had built a large well-equipped militia and its governor, Imanuel Gonzales Cosco, refused to disband it. According to a report from the acting president, Miguel Barragan, Zacatecas had amassed eighteen battalions of infantry, nine regiments of cavalry, and numerous pieces of artillery. All told, he estimated that the state could field a twenty-thousand-man army if the entire force was called out. In early March 1835, Barragan issued orders to units of the national army and state militias loyal to the government to begin preparing for a possible campaign to bring Zacatecas into compliance with the Centralist designs. On March 31, the national government issued a decree ordering the states' militias reduced in size. In anticipation of the announcement, the state legislature had declared the day before (March 30) that the governor had the power to call out the militia to resist the national government's plan.

Barragan ordered the assembled troops (designated the Army of the North) to march on Zacatecas. Antonio López de Santa Anna, who had returned home and left the government in Barragan's hands, agreed to command the expedition. The force totaled approximately 3,500, composed of 2,200 infantrymen organized into two divisions, 1,000 cavalry organized into one division, and 172 sappers, who made up part of the Reserve Division. The column possessed 18 pieces of artillery manned by 140 artillerymen. Santa Anna marshaled his troops throughout April, advancing toward Zacatecas around the first of May.

Santa Anna approached Zacatecas on the afternoon of May 10, 1835. The terrain consisted of a series of ravines that deeply cut what had once been a broad plateau into numerous hills and ridges. South of the capital lay the village of Guadalupe, which blocked a ravine leading to Zacatecas. The general conducted a reconnaissance of the rebel defenses and learned that the main body of the Zacatecan militia had been positioned on the western outskirts of Guadalupe, using the village to secure their left flank. Earthworks had been built further up the ravine to halt any Centralist troops that might break through the main line of battle. Several redoubts had been built on the hills to the east overlooking Zacatecas to serve as a line of last defense. Francisco Garcia, who had been named commander of the rebel forces by Gonzales Cosio, had decided that he would wait for an attack and rely on his defenses to defeat Santa Anna.

Santa Anna developed a typical Napoleonic strategy to defeat the Zacatecans. The 1st Brigade of the First Infantry Division was ordered to assault the rebel's main line while the 2nd Brigade assaulted the militiamen that occupied the village of Guadalupe; elements of the Centralist artillery were to assist in the attack. Once the main body of the rebels was engaged, Santa Anna planned to march the 2nd Infantry Division east of Guadalupe and envelop the enemy's left flank. Once the rebels at Guadalupe were defeated, Santa Anna and his troops could advance on the capital.

The battle commenced shortly before the sun rose. The Centralists made steady headway against the militiamen, although Santa Anna's 2nd Infantry Division initially encountered more resistance than expected. He was helped by the arrival of his Cavalry Division when it swung around his right flank and dashed behind the rebels' lines. With the route to Zacatecas cut, many of the militiamen abandoned their defenses in and around Guadalupe and raced up the ravine road toward the capital in panic and into the hands of the Centralists. The battle disintegrated into a rout as Santa Anna's Reserve Division joined in the chase. In just over an hour, the Centralists had smashed the famed Zacatecan Militia and were at the gates of the state capital. Santa Anna and his troops entered Zacatecas with little trouble, having either killed, captured, or dispersed the city's defenders.

Santa Anna's political enemies charged that he unleashed his troops on the capital where they enjoyed a looting spree that reportedly lasted several days: the affair was labeled the "Rape of Zacatecas." Revenge reportedly was not the only motive—the destruction of property and abuse suffered by the former rebels served as a stern warning for other Mexicans contemplating revolt. The commander-in-chief soon withdrew from the scene but not before naming his cavalry commander, General Joaquín Ramírez y Sesma as Commanding General of Zacatecas. By June, Governor Gonzales formally surrendered to the national authorities, an act that helped to restore order within the rebellious state.

Proponents of the militia tradition looked for an explanation as to why this supposedly well-trained and well-equipped army of citizen-soldiers failed to live up to the high expectations placed on it. One rebel who survived the battle, a German mining engineer named Eduard Harkort whose aid had been enlisted by Governor Gonzales, blamed the defeat on the rebel commander, García, who lacked military training. He charged that García fled the field after the opening shots, followed by his troops whom he had poorly positioned. Others claimed that Santa Anna secretly planned for one or more of his officers to pretend to join the rebels on the eve of the battle. The defectors, trained soldiers, were given important commands in the Zacatecan militia. These spies then deliberately positioned their troops in disadvantageous places from which they could not fend off the attack. Whether or not these claims were valid, the fact remained that Zacatecan militia failed to stand up to a professional army.

The Centralist government had already made plans to address the trouble brewing in Coahuila y Tejas. Unlike Zacatecas, where the citizens had been predominately supporters of the federal republic, the populace in Coahuila y Tejas had split into Federalist and Centralist factions. The hostilities there actually predated the Plan of Cuernavaca. The dispute originated with the adoption of the federal constitution and its denial of separate statehood for Texas. National officials believed that Texas lacked sufficient population and economic development to warrant statehood and therefore attached it to

Coahuila as a department within that state. Texas, which until then had enjoyed the same political status as its neighbor, felt slighted. The denial of statehood not only meant the loss of political autonomy, it also was viewed as an economic disadvantage. This was a sore point with the Texans, both Anglo and native-born, prior to Santa Anna's rejection of federalism.[2]

Texas, as represented by its settlements, had developed two distinct populations. The first was native, made up of people who had been born either under the Spanish or Mexican flag. The other was Anglo, composed of colonists who had emigrated to Texas from the United States. This is not to say that there was no interaction or common interest between these two groups. Many native-born Texans appreciated and counted on the economic development sparked by the arrival of these industrious Americans. Texas, a frontier region that shared a border with the United States, had enjoyed an illicit trade with Americans for years. Hence, the existing economic ties between American businessmen and native-born Texans were reinforced by the emerging commercial interests of the newcomers.

Trouble had erupted in the summer of 1832 between American colonists and government officials. Tax exemptions that had been granted the colonists had elapsed. One section of the Law of April 6, 1830, had called for the national government to establish garrisons across Texas and to open customhouses. The measures were intended to curtail smuggling and to regulate trade so taxes could be collected and revenues generated. A customhouse was established on the coast near the spot where the Trinity River flows into the gulf. Construction on Fort Anahuac began in late 1830. The colonists resented the efforts of the fort's commander, a Kentuckian named Juan Davis Bradburn, to enforce the government's laws regulating commerce. In June 1832, Colonel Bradburn arrested two colonists for their anti-government activities. Friends of William B. Travis and Patrick Jack—the two men imprisoned by Bradburn—came to their aid and forced the garrison's commander to release them. A skirmish also erupted at the nearby port of Velasco between the colonists and government troops. The colonists, who learned that Santa Anna had revolted against an unpopular Centralist administration, claimed that their action against

48

Bradburn had been carried out in support of the broader Federalist revolution. Their explanation satisfied General José Antonio Mexía who had been sent to Texas to investigate the incident. Mexía left Texas with his troops to join Santa Anna. The emergency had passed but important issues still remained unresolved.

The colonists, many of whom realized that they had narrowly averted a military occupation of their settlements, determined to try a more diplomatic approach by which they could address their needs. In October 1832, fifty-five delegates met at San Felipe to petition the national government to hear their concerns. They requested renewal of the tax exemptions, an end to the ban on immigration from the United States, swifter granting of land titles, and most radical of all, separate statehood for Texas. Stephen F. Austin believed that the colonists were moving too quickly in their demands, an opinion held by the residents of Tejano population centers such as Béxar. They did not necessarily disapprove of the ideas advanced by the colonists, but political activism of this type had not been widely practiced under Spanish rule. The movement died without Austin's support.

The colonists gathered at San Felipe again in April 1833, determined to present their demands to the government. This time Austin reluctantly agreed to carry their petition to Mexico City, which contained a newly drafted state constitution just in case statehood was granted. Austin arrived at the national capital and began calling on his political allies in order to press the colonists' case for change. He was able to have the ban on immigration modified, but he met little success on the matter of Texas statehood. Frustrated, he wrote an uncharacteristically strong letter to his supporters in Texas in which he instructed them to proceed with the plan for statehood. The *empresario* then left Mexico City and headed home. Officials in Béxar read the letter, became alarmed at its tone, and returned it to authorities in Mexico City. Austin was arrested and imprisoned for more than a year before being allowed to return to Texas.

Although the colonists and native-born Texans were split over how to approach the national government on the issue of statehood, the Department of Texas had been able to forge an alliance with a powerful faction located at Monclova that was ready to challenge Saltillo for control of the existing state of Coahuila y Tejas. In 1833, representatives from Monclova and Texas were able to pass legislation changing the capital of the state from Saltillo to Monclova. Thus, the state was already involved in a local political feud when the Centralist assault on the federal republic occurred. The outbreak of the civil war, occasioned by Santa Anna's backing of The Plan of Cuernavaca, drove the political factions in Coahuila y Tejas even further apart and caused them to take sides in the emerging national conflict. Saltillo accepted Santa Anna and the dismantling of the federal republic but Monclova and the Department of Texas opposed the change. The stage was set for what historians in the United States have labeled the "Texas Revolution."

WAR COMES TO TEXAS

Several events occurred in the summer of 1835 that brought Texas closer to revolt. Rebellious colonists once more confronted the Centralist garrison at Anahuac. The national government, fresh from its victory over the Zacatecans, cracked down on the federalist junta at Monclova in Coahuila. Plans were also made, once this new rebellion had been suppressed, to exert control over the seemingly ungrateful colonists in Texas. Austin, finally allowed to leave Mexico City, returned home to find Texas in turmoil. The storm was about to break.

The first rumbles occurred at Fort Anahuac, whose garrison had been withdrawn following the 1832 disturbance there but subsequently had been reactivated. The national government instructed the post's new commander, Captain Antonio Tenorio, to collect taxes from merchants importing goods into Texas. One merchant, Andrew Briscoe, challenged Tenorio's authority and on June 12 was arrested by the captain. William B. Travis, who had been at the center of the 1832 disturbance, responded to the government's action by raising a company of volunteers and marching on Anahuac. On June 20, Tenorio surrendered the fort to Travis and retired to San Felipe with his soldiers.

Instead of receiving praise from his fellow colonists, however, Travis discovered that the majority of them believed he had acted rashly and condemned his actions. Tenorio and his men were treated to a public dinner by the residents of San Felipe. Travis, whose action had outpaced public support, found himself out of step with his neighbors and issued a statement that many took as an apology, although he told his neighbors, "Time alone will show whether the step was correct or not."[3] The assault on the Centralist garrison added to the growing tension in northern Mexico.

While Santa Anna put down the revolt in Zacatecas, General Martín Perfecto de Cos dealt with the rebellious Monclova federalist faction. Coahuila's militia had been ordered to go home. On April 14, Augustín Viesca, who opposed the Plan of Cuernavaca, was sworn in the state's new governor. One week later, the state legislature disbanded under pressure from Cos. Before leaving, though, legislators granted Viesca the authority to relocate the capital to a place of his choosing. The governor designated Béxar the new capital of Coahuila y Tejas and attempted to remove the archives to that place, putting distance between his Federalist government and its Centralist opponents. He and a party of his supporters were captured on June 8 and subsequently imprisoned at Monterey.

The breakup of the legislature and Viecsa's capture left Cos in charge of Coahuila y Tejas. He now acted to bring the dissidents in Texas under control. Orders were issued to send troops there to strengthen the government's presence. The small, isolated garrisons of the past were to be replaced with large concentrations of Centralist soldiers. Moreover, orders went out to arrest troublemakers like the colonist Travis and Lorenzo de Zavala, a well-known national political figure who opposed the Centralists and was then living in Texas. News of Cos's plans brought forth cries that the Centralists were planning to cast a military despotism over Texas. Samuel M. Williams, Austin's business partner, informed the citizens of San Felipe that correspondence had been found in the possession of Centralist spies in which Cos disclosed that troops were already on their way to Texas and more could be expected. According to Colonel Domingo de Ugartachea, the military commander at Béxar,

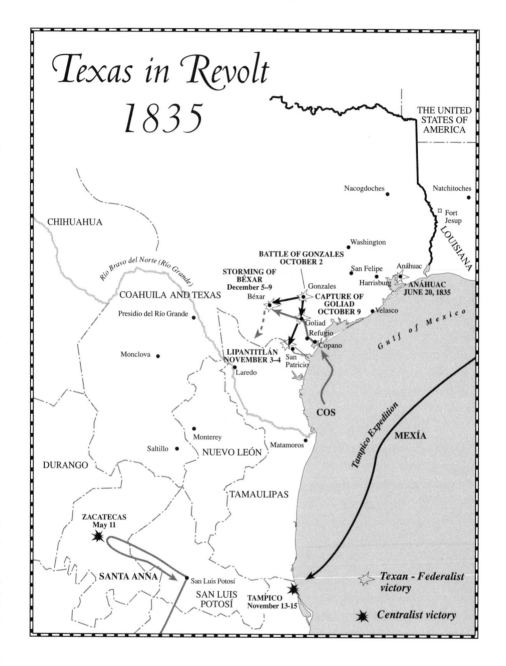

Texas in Revolt 1835

THE UNITED STATES OF AMERICA

Nacogdoches •

Natchitoches •

⊡ Fort Jesup

CHIHUAHUA

LOUISIANA

Washington •

Río Bravo del Norte (Río Grande)

BATTLE OF GONZALES OCTOBER 2

San Felipe • Anáhuac •

STORMING OF BÉXAR December 5–9

Gonzales

Harrisburg •

ANÁHUAC JUNE 20, 1835

COAHUILA AND TEXAS

Béxar •

CAPTURE OF GOLIAD OCTOBER 9

Velasco •

Presidio del Río Grande •

Goliad •

Refugio •

Gu l f o f M e x i c o

Monclova •

LIPANTITLÁN NOVEMBER 3–4

San Patricio

Copano

Laredo •

COS

Tampico Expedition

MEXÍA

Monterey •

Saltillo •

Matamoros •

DURANGO

NUEVO LEÓN

TAMAULIPAS

ZACATECAS May 11

SANTA ANNA

San Luis Potosí •

SAN LUIS POTOSÍ

TAMPICO November 13-15

Texan - Federalist victory

✸ *Centralist victory*

52

"the business of Texas will soon be regulated, as the government has ordered a large division composed of the troops that went against Zaccatecas, to Texas and which are now at Saltillo; that force is three thousand four hundred men."[4] The colonists formed committees of public safety as a way to organize resistance, but few agreed with Williams's call for an immediate march on Béxar.

Austin finally returned to Texas. Oddly enough, his release had been arranged by Santa Anna, who apparently believed the *empresario* would have a calming effect on the colonists. Austin arrived to find that two distinct political factions had emerged in Texas in his absence. The War Party, as the name indicated, contended that the Centralists' onslaught on the federal republic needed to be met with force. The other faction, the Peace Party, still held out hope that there would be a diplomatic solution to the crisis. Additionally, the Peace Party believed that any action taken against the government must be carried out with the support and approval of other Mexican Federalists outside of Texas. Cooperation, they explained, would serve two purposes; first, additional resources could be brought against the Centralists, and second, it would deflect charges that the struggle was merely an Anglo attempt to sever Texas from Mexico. Austin, who had been closely allied to the men who made up the Peace Party before his imprisonment, returned home convinced that the time had passed for peaceful overtures and that Texas must prepare to defend itself from the coming onslaught. Austin's shift mirrored a growing militancy in Texas that made war with the Centralists almost inevitable.

The situation reminded colonists of their own revolutionary past. Comparisons were made between British oppression in 1775 and similar actions that had been initiated by Mexico's Centralists. Communities resorted to the same methods of communication by forming Committees of Public Safety to keep each other informed of new developments. Oddly, they did not see opposition to the national government as radical but as conservative. Wrote one colonist, "Ours is not a rebellious or revolutionary or voluntary warfare. It has been forced upon us. Justice, liberty, & the constitution, & the god of battles are on our side and the proud and imperious Dictator, Santa

Anna, will be made to feel and know from blood bought experience, that a people who have adopted the motto of their ancestors, 'Liberty or Death,' will crush & laugh [at] his tyranny to enslave them."[5]

The news that Cos was on the way to Texas to reinforce the garrison at Béxar electrified the colonists. Already on edge, a demand from that post's garrison commander, Colonel Domingo de Ugartechea, further alarmed the citizens of Gonzales. The government had issued a small cannon to the town several years before to be used for defense against Indian raiders. Ugartechea sent Lieutenant Francisco de Castañeda with approximately one hundred members of the Presidial Company of Alamo de Parras to reclaim the gun as part of the Centralists' reduction of the state militias and the confiscation of any associated weapons. Moreover, with the current political unrest in Texas, why leave arms in the hands of the colonists that could be used against the government?

To the Americans, however, the military's action conjured up images of the English march on Lexington and Concord. Approximately 140 colonists gathered at Gonzales, determined to prevent the gun's removal. They elected John Henry Moore their leader and carried a white homemade banner bearing a representation of the disputed cannon and the words "Come and Take It." On the morning of October 2, 1835, the colonists fired on Castañeda and his men when they approached. The colonists suffered no losses but reportedly found blood on the ground occupied by the Centralists, who broke off the skirmish and returned to Béxar. Although a minor military engagement, the skirmish on the banks of the Guadalupe River proved to be the opening battle of the war.

On October 4, Austin reported to the San Felipe Committee of Public Safety that "War is declared—public opinion has proclaimed it against a Military despotism—The campaign has commenced—The Military have advanced to Gonzales—Gen Cos has arrived and threatens to overrun the country." He concluded that "one spirit and one purpose animates the people of this part of the country, and that is to take Béxar, and drive the Military out of Texas."[6] His business partner, Williams, had expressed the opinion back in June that Béxar should be captured, but his fellow colonists thought the act too precipitous then. With shots fired, all minds now turned toward Béxar and driving Cos out of Texas. Word went out and colonists began to flock to Gonzales for the coming campaign.

The next engagement occurred further south, even as volunteers gathered at Gonzales. The town of Goliad was located near an old Spanish fort called Presidio La Bahía. The fort, overlooking the crossing on the San Antonio River, guarded the road to Béxar. Cos had passed through Goliad in late September on his way to reinforce Urgartechea. If La Bahía could be captured, not only would a Centralist outpost be eliminated, but Béxar would be cut off from the coast. Captain Manuel Sabriego commanded the stronghold and its garrison of seventy-five Centralist soldiers and local ranchers. On the night of October 9, 1835, George M. Collinsworth and approximately 120 colonists surprised and captured the fort after a brief fight. As at Gonzales, the colonists suffered no losses. They reported that three Centralist soldiers had been killed, seven wounded, and another twenty-one taken prisoner. As an additional prize, the colonists captured a large cache of weapons, ammunition, and other military supplies.

Meanwhile, the colonists at Gonzales organized themselves into the Army of the People, and unanimously elected Austin their commander in chief. On October 11, Austin issued his first order in which he appointed his staff officers and announced that the army would assemble at 9 AM the following day, ready to commence the march to Béxar. He used the occasion to set the tone he hoped would be established for the campaign:

> the Commander in chief deems it his duty to remind each citizen soldier that patriotism and firmness will but little avail, without discipline and strict obedience to orders. The first duty of a soldier is obedience. It is expected that the army of the people altho hastily collected will present an example of obedience that will do honor to the cause we are engaged in, and credit to the patriots who are defending it.

Austin was to be disappointed and frustrated with his citizen-soldiers, but he understood them and always believed they were up to the task of taking Béxar.

Austin's army crossed the Guadalupe the next day but did not actually start for Béxar until October 14. In the meantime, Austin had ordered an election for field officers for the nearly three hundred men who comprised the battalion of volunteers under his command. John H. Moore, who had commanded the colonists in their October 2 action, was elected colonel; Edward Burleson, a colonist with a reputation as an Indian fighter, was elected lieutenant colonel; and Alexander Somerville was elected major. Austin appointed Benjamin Rush Milam, who had been in Texas longer than many of his fellow colonists, captain of a spy company. He issued more orders to the army, instructing the men not to fire while on the march, to hobble or tie up their horses when the army stopped for the night, and have their weapons in good repair at all times. Companies had to have at least thirty men but could be as large as seventy. Every volunteer had to belong to an organized company in order to promote order. He further warned, "All riotous conduct and noisy clamorous talk is specially prohibited."[7]

Austin's army at this point was composed entirely of colonists who had volunteered to march on Béxar. Benjamin F. Smith, an acquaintance of Austin's, shared his experience with citizens-soldiers and warned him to move quickly or he could expect trouble. He wrote, "When I wrote you yesterday it was my desire to have urged you to order [the march] immediately because I know Militia could not be kept at a post like this [Gonzales] long at a time—and in this I was correct." Smith, who had been left in charge of the volunteers at La Bahía, correctly summarized Austin's predicament and what lay ahead for him when he warned, "take warning by this mishap you are not on a bed of roses—and if you are compelled to stay long at a place; rely upon it, your men will desert you—There is nothing but their honor to govern them—this is in many cases but a *cobweb*."[8]

The Army of the People had reached Cibolo Creek several miles east of Béxar by October 16. Austin sent Cos a message proposing a meeting he believed would open the way "for a satisfactory adjustment of all the affairs of Texas." Cos responded by saying that as hostilities had commenced, and Austin was at the head of an illegal force operating against the national government, that no meeting could take place between them. Austin's description of the colonists camped on the Cibolo as the "Division of the Federal Army of Texas" drew Cos's ire, prompting the Centralist general to tell the *empresario* that Mexico only had one army in Texas and he, not Austin, commanded it. Events had proceeded to the point that the chance of a peaceful solution evaporated.

As predicted, the Army of the People began to show signs of indecision. On October 18, Austin wrote the Committee of Public Safety at San Felipe to inform them that Cos and his soldiers, who had learned of the capture of La Bahía, had been "busily engaged in fortifying S. Antonio, barricading the streets, placing cannon on the top of the church cutting down trees, and in evry way exerting themselves to make a vigorous defense." As for his volunteers, he said, "The army is in high spirits and eager to advance, but are at the same time not disposed to act precipitatley or rashly."[9] Austin held a council of war with his officers to determine whether to wait for reinforcements or continue the advance on Béxar. The group determined to wait. The next day, however, the council reassembled and reversed its decision, giving their commander the discretion to advance. Austin moved his army forward, halting on the bank of Salado Creek only five miles from Béxar and in sight of Cos's pickets.

Austin spent the next few days securing his camp and waiting for men and supplies to come up from Gonzales, Goliad, Nacogdoches, and other settlements. He ordered Colonel James Bowie (an honorary title he had held in recognition of his previous campaigns and who was acting as inspector general) to accompany Captain James W. Fannin and his men on a scout of the missions south of Béxar to look for corn, beans, and information. Austin also appointed Juan N. Seguín—a prominent local resident and "devoted friend of the Constitution"—to the rank of "Captn. of the Federal Army" with instruction to raise a company of "Mexicans" from the area's ranches and mission.[10] Reinforcements trickled in, slowly increasing the number of colonists gathered before Béxar.

On October 24, Austin informed the Committee of Public Safety at San Felipe that he had that day "commenced the investment of San Antonio" and believed it could be taken in a few days if the expected reinforcements were hastened forward quickly. Skirmishes had occurred every day since his army's arrival on Salado Creek. Several *soldados* had come into camp as deserters. Seguín assured him that the townspeople favored the Federalist cause, leading him to expect their assistance in an attack on Béxar. Over the next few days, reinforcements were directed to the army's camps at the old missions at San José and Espada. One well-known colonist, William B. Travis, arrived and was appointed lieutenant by Austin and authorized to raise a company of volunteer cavalry.[11] Austin constantly reminded his officers of their duty to enforce discipline and his soldiers that it was their duty to obey.

Events appeared to be building for a clash. On October 27, Austin ordered Bowie to accompany Fannin and several companies in a northward advance toward Béxar to locate a suitable campsite for the army. Austin, who intended to bring up the army that evening, was unable to do so. Bowie and Fannin had selected a bend in the San Antonio River in sight of Mission Concepción. October 28 dawned foggy. Cos, they learned, had sent out a detachment of approximately three hundred cavalry and infantry with two pieces of artillery to drive the rebels away. Bowie and Fannin positioned their men, who numbered about ninety, along the river where they could take cover on its tree-lined banks. Ugartechea, who commanded the Centralists, ordered his troops to assault the colonists. Several attempts were made but the fire from the concealed rebels inflicted a number of casualties on them and broke up the attacks. Ugartechea withdrew to town, leaving some sixteen dead and one of his cannon on the field. Austin had tried to reach the scene while the fighting still raged but arrived after the Centralists had broken off the engagement. He wanted to follow up the victory and mount an immediate attack on the town, but his officers advised him not to take such a bold step. Thus, although the Centralists were unable to break the siege, the colonists possibly missed the opportunity to seize the town from a shaken enemy.

An easy victory over the Centralists became less certain in November, despite the drubbing they had taken at the Battle of Concepción. Cos could not drive Austin away, but Austin could not enter the town. The siege seemed to lose momentum even though the colonists gained several more small victories over Cos's men. Travis's cavalry company captured a horse herd belonging to the Centralist garrison that had been pastured some distance from the city. Although the most of the animals were unserviceable, their seizure deprived Cos of this valuable asset. On November 26, Bowie commanded a detachment that intercepted a pack train that was attempting to deliver fodder and other supplies to Béxar. The skirmish, known as the "Grass Fight," took place on Alazan Creek west of town and resulted in the train's capture and the loss of three Centralist soldiers and another fourteen wounded. Unable to take the town by force, Austin attempted to starve Cos into submission.

Events happening elsewhere that November would affect the course and conduct of the war. Another Centralist garrison remained in Texas in addition to the one at Béxar. Situated on the Nueces River south of Goliad, Lipantitlan was one of the forts established by the Law of April 6, 1830. On November 3, Captain Ira J. Westover led some seventy colonists in an assault on the fort. The post was defended by Captain Nicolás Rodríguez, who had approximately ninety soldiers under his command. The rebels overran the fort but were forced to abandon it the next day when the government troops received reinforcements. Although twenty-eight Centralist soldiers reportedly died in the affair, the heavy resistance encountered by the colonists revealed that Centralist sentiment remained strong in the area below Goliad.

The most significant event at this time did not occur in Texas at all but took place in Tampico in the Mexican state of Tamaulipas. The idea of cooperating with other Mexican Federalists still had supporters. Earlier in the revolt, a meeting was held in New Orleans between three prominent exiled Federalists: former Vice President Valentín Gómez Farías, General José Antonio Mexía, and former Governor Lorenzo de Zavala. Desiring an expanded front against the Centralists, they decided to send an expedition to seize the port of

Tampico to bolster Federalist support there. In October, Mexía raised about 150 volunteers (some foreign but most American), bought arms and other military equipment, and chartered a ship. Once under sail, he informed his recruits of their destination and persuaded them to participate in the attack on the city. One American volunteer later related what happened: "the object of the men on Board was to Go to Texas to Volenteer in ade of the Caus of Liberty. . . . the men began to grow oneasy [as to where] we ware goin - we was Bound to Brasorah [Brazoria] when we Started in[to] Texes, but we was informed that we ware goin to Tampeco in Mexico." The group finally assented to the invasion. He continued, "We would have to Lan But we Should Shurley take the town without much troble wen we would get plenty of Gold. With theas and maney more fair promises we at Last Consented to go for there [was] no other alturnitive for us."[12] The expedition arrived at Tampico during a storm and their ship ran aground, soaking the men and spoiling the expedition's ammunition. Despite word that the Centralists remained in firm control of the city, Mexía decided to proceed with the attack. The volunteers made their advance on the night of November 15 but were soon driven off. Mexía loaded his survivors onto another ship and sailed for Texas.

The Centralist response to the attack set an important precedent. Thirty-one volunteers had been captured and the authorities at Tampico wondered what should be done with these prisoners. Word arrived from Santa Anna that these men should be considered pirates and dealt with accordingly because Mexico was not currently at war with any nation. Three of the volunteers had already died of their wounds but the remaining twenty-eight were placed before a firing squad and executed. This policy, later formally adopted by the national congress, established that "no quarter" would be given by the Centralist government in its campaign to crush the revolt in Texas.

Mexía's defeat seriously threatened future cooperation between the Federalists in Texas and other parts of Mexico. So did an incident that occurred at Goliad that same month. Governor Viesca and his party, who had been captured by Cos's men, had been held in prison at Monterey since June. In late October orders came to transfer the prisoners to San Jun de Ulúa, a fortress at the port city of Vera Cruz. In an odd turn of events, Lieutenant Colonel José Maria Gonzales, who commanded the detail guarding Viesca, pronounced in favor of the revolt and set off with the governor for Texas. Viesca arrived at Goliad expecting to be received with all the pomp and respect due his office, but a cold reception awaited him. The post's commander, Captain Philip Dimmit, and his men refused to recognize Viesca's authority. Moreover, Dimitt refused Gonzales's offer to place himself and his men in the of service of Texas. The dream of a Federalist coalition was seriously damaged and would only deteriorate in the coming weeks.

VICTORY AT BÉXAR

The Army of the People lost its commander in November. Delegates meeting at San Felipe decided that Austin should go to the United States to rally support for the war in Texas. On November 18, Austin received news of his appointment. He replied he was ready to accept the assignment but cautioned "Some prudence will be necessary to keep this army together should I leave at once."[13] Frustrated at not having yet taken Béxar, on November 21 Austin issued orders for an attack on the city in hopes of achieving his goal before withdrawing from the army. He was to be disappointed once more when his officers informed him that the majority of their men were unwilling to undertake the attack. Austin informed the Provisional Government that the siege would continue but they must forward flour, corn, sea biscuits, and beans to feed the troops. On November 24, Austin reviewed the Army of the People for the last time. The volunteers elected Edward Burleson as Austin's successor. The change was an important development that marked a new phase in the war.

Prior to Austin's departure, a canvass was held to determine how many of the troops camped outside Béxar were willing to stay and maintain the siege; 405 men agreed to remain. Not all of these men were colonists, though. On November 22, Austin reported that a company of volunteers from New Orleans had arrived in camp. No longer would the war just be an affair between Mexican Federalists and Centralists. The tone and goal of the war changed as colonists began to leave the field, their places taken by American volunteers who were arriving from the United States in increasing numbers.

Burleson inherited what amounted to a collection of independent companies instead of a unified command. Many colonists believed that the siege should be broken off and the army reassembled in the spring for another campaign. Men began to abandon camp, some saying they were going after warmer clothing and supplies, others just leaving without offering any explanation. Needing to make use of those troops who still remained, Burleson ordered an assault on the city scheduled for the morning of December 4. Like Austin, Burleson found that the men were unwilling to undertake the attack. At this point his choices were to maintain the siege with a force that was on the verge of disbanding or to end the siege and withdraw to the east.

Not everyone in camp was willing to abandon the siege they had supported for nearly six weeks. The newly arrived New Orleans Greys had come to fight and voiced their support for an attack on Cos. Some of the men who had started the campaign at Gonzales also objected. William Carey, who was later to die at the Alamo, told his sister what happened when Burleson announced the withdrawal:

> on the 4th day of December a retreat was ordered to the satisfaction of many but to the grief of a few brave souls who was among the first that volunteered and who preferred Death in the cause rather than such a disgraceful retreat. We rallied around a brave soul (Colo Milan) and requested him to be our leader, he consented and 150 of us declared to take the place or die in the attempt, while a large number of them endeavored to discourage us and said we would all be butchered, but a few more seen we were resolute and joined untill our number was 220, and on the next morning about day break we marched in the town under the heavy fires of their cannon & musketry, . . .[14]

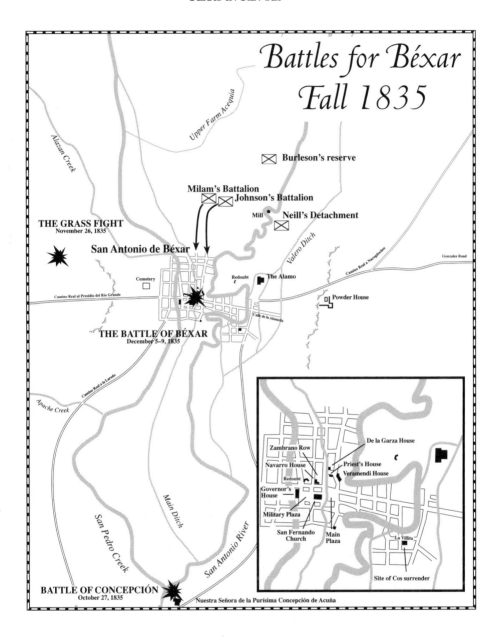

Battles for Béxar Fall 1835

Burleson's reserve

Milam's Battalion
Johnson's Battalion

Mill

Neill's Detachment

THE GRASS FIGHT
November 26, 1835

San Antonio de Béxar

Upper Farm Acequia

Alazan Creek

Valero Ditch

Camino Real a Nacogdoches

Gonzales Road

Cemetery

Redoubt

The Alamo

Camino Real al Presidio del Rio Grande

Powder House

Calle de la Alameda

THE BATTLE OF BÉXAR
December 5–9, 1835

Camino Real a la Laredo

Apache Creek

Main Ditch

San Pedro Creek

BATTLE OF CONCEPCIÓN
October 27, 1835

San Antonio River

Nuestra Señora de la Purísima Concepción de Acuña

Zambrano Row

De la Garza House

Navarro House

Priest's House
Veramendi House

Redoubt

Governor's
House

Military Plaza

San Fernando
Church

Main
Plaza

La Villita

Site of Cos surrender

The daring assault was made possible because Burleson declared that he would hold the remaining men in reserve to safeguard the attackers' rear and flanks as they advanced. James C. Neill, who commanded the artillery for the rebels, supported the assault with fire from his battery. The attackers were organized into two columns, one commanded by Milam and the other led by Frank W. Johnson, Burleson's adjutant and inspector general. Many in the rebel camp were relieved that action was finally being taken to break the stalemate.

On the morning of December 5, the two columns entered the town from the north using two separate streets that led to the central plaza. The ensuing battle lasted for five days, with fierce fighting from house to house. On December 7, a Centralist bullet killed Milam and his command fell to Robert C. Morris, an officer of the New Olreans Greys. On December 8, 650 Centralist reinforcements arrived, raising Cos's total force to around 1250. These men were of little use, though, as most of them were untrained recruits whose arrival doubled the demand on his already inadequate food supply. On December 9, rebel gains around the central plaza coupled with the defection of several companies of presidial troops convinced Cos to end the battle and open talks for the surrender of the town. The capitulation was formalized on December 10 in a brief meeting where both commanders signed the surrender document. Centralist casualties reportedly amounted to some one hundred killed, wounded, and missing. The rebels had five or six killed and had twenty-five to thirty wounded in the fighting.

Lieutenant Carey provided details of the Battle of Béxar to his family, writing "we succeeded in getting possession of some stone houses (which is outside of the square) that sheltered us a little from their fires until we could make Breastworks for ourselves we labored hard day and night for 5 days still gaining possession when on the morning of the 5th day they sent in a flag of truce to the extreme joy of us all." The fight was made all the more desperate because "The enemy on the third day of the siege raised a black flag (which says no quarters)." As for his participation in the battle, he informed them "I thought & still think that nothing but fate saved [me] . . . two of the killed received the shots along side of me when discharging their duty at a cannon . . . when the men was killed & wounded I loaded and fired the gun assisted by two more instead of ten and escaped only slightly wounded, a ball passed through my hat and cut the flesh to the scull bone and my clothes received many shots until by a lucky shot made by me into the port-hole of the Enemy I dismounted their cannon which caused them to cease firing . . . the wound never prevented me from working the guns."[15] Carey believed that the treaty ending the battle was unnecessary and called it a "childs bargain." He and other volunteers believed the fighting should have continued until the Centralists were completely routed.

Burleson and Cos had appointed representatives to work out the specific terms of the Centralist surrender. Their goal was to prevent "the further effusion of blood, and the ravages of civil war." The document contained eighteen articles that governed the Centralist turnover of the town and its public works. One of the most important of these stated that "general Cos and his officers retire into the interior of the republic, under parole of honor; that they will not in any way oppose the re-establishment of the federal Constitution of 1824."[16] The rebels based their treatment of Cos and his men on accepted practices most countries had adopted regarding prisoners of war. According to *General Regulations for the [U. S.] Army for 1821*, "Prisoners taken from the enemy, from the moment that they yield themselves, as long as they obey the necessary orders given them, are under the safeguard of the national faith and honour. They will be treated at all times with every indulgence not inconsistent with their safe-keeping, and with good order among them." Prisoners of war released on parole would not take up arms against the victors until a proper exchange was arranged between their respective governments. Punishment for breaking one's parole would result in the prisoner being placed in chains although the government could issue other orders or follow the example set by the "usages of war."[17] It was thought that an enemy, if treated well, would return the favor should the role of captor and prisoner be reversed. Not happy with the treaty, some volunteers warned that Cos had no intention of accepting a parole and that he would return to fight another day—a warning that went unheeded.

The fall offensive had gone extremely well for the colonists. With Cos's capitulation, the rebels now controlled Béxar and effectively had cleared Texas of all significant Centralist garrisons. The question remained: Would they be prepared for the Mexican government's response to this challenge to its authority?

Chapter Four
Texas in Turmoil

When a nation is without establishments and a military system,
it is very difficult to organize an army.[1]
Napoleon
Maxims

The men of the Béxar garrison had retired for the night still confident in their own fighting ability. They had grown up hearing tales of their fathers' and grandfathers' struggles against the English and their Indian allies. Many had lived on the frontier where vigilance was the watchword. Military service was not only considered a civil duty, it was an honor, too. Without time to build a regular army, the rebels depended on the citizen-soldier to throw back the advancing Centralist army. Had not Jackson proved at New Orleans that a hastily thrown together force of frontiersmen could stand up against hardened British veterans of the wars against Napoleon? Some volunteers at Béxar boasted that a single American could lick ten Mexicans. That boast was about to be put to the test.

Santa Anna equally had little doubt that his *soldados* would overcome these rank amateurs before him. He had boasted that he would drive the foreigners into Louisiana and follow them clear to Washington City. Although some of his troops were new conscripts, he had many veterans hardened by previous campaigns. He also had experienced officers. This battle would show the rebels that frontier rabble was no match for a professional army. There was a lesson to be taught here and he was an eager taskmaster. The time had almost arrived to launch the attack and reclaim the Alamo.

THE ATTEMPT TO BUILD A REGULAR ARMY

The outbreak of hostilities had forced the colonists to scramble to field an army. They drew on their previous experience in dealing with emergencies by depending on the community to provide citizens-soldiers as the bulwark of their defense. Many realized, however, that Texas needed a regular army if the revolution were to be sustained for any length of time. The rush to form an army unleashed chaos as various revolutionary factions argued over its composition, vied for its control, and differed over how it should be used.

The men who turned out in the fall of 1835 followed the frontier military tradition with which they were familiar. Ad hoc military companies were formed by volunteers who responded to the calls of local leaders. These companies were consisted predominantly of men from Anglo communities within the colonies. No specific term of service was designated; the companies were task oriented. In October 1835, enough companies gathered at Gonzales to form a battalion set to march on Béxar. Before departing camp, the volunteers of the battalion unanimously named Austin commander-in-chief of what was termed the Army of the People. The democratic conclave granted Austin authority but empowered their officers to represent their wishes in councils of war, providing a check on orders they disliked. Productive members of their community, many of these citizen-soldiers eventually returned home with fighting still to be done.

Earlier that summer, colonists elected delegates to serve at a meeting styled the Consultation, a meeting to discuss what course of action Texas should take to counter recent developments. They began arriving at Gonzales, the town designated for this important gathering, in mid-October. The meeting had originally been called to discuss possible hostilities, but the delegates now had to face the reality that war had arrived. Immediate action had to be taken to form a revolutionary government and an army to support it. Notwithstanding this urgent need, the men of the Army of the People demanded that the delegates accompany them to Béxar. So many delegates agreed to go with the army that the Consultation had to be rescheduled for San Felipe for November 1, 1835. It took until November 3 for a quorum to be formed before the Consultation could start work on creating a civic and military framework for the revolution.

One of the first orders of business was to explain to the public why Texas was engaged in a revolt against the national government. It quickly became apparent that the Peace Party and the War Party had different views on the subject. Adherents of the Peace Party believed that an attempt should be made to cooperate with other Mexican Federalists in order to present the conflict to the world as a dispute between Mexico's political factions over the fate of the Constitution of 1824. They contended that war was being fought to restore the federal republic. The War Party, however, believed that Texas's future should not be tied in any way to Mexico and contended that the current hostility was in reality a war for independence. The Peace Party claimed support for the war would come from other Mexican Federalists while the War Party claimed an outright declaration of independence would bring even more aid from the United States.

On November 7, 1835, the Consultation issued a proclamation called the Declaration of Causes that stated Texas was defending "the republican principles of the federal constitution of Mexico, of eighteen and twenty-four." Although it appeared that the Peace Party had won, the declaration was actually a compromise that contended Texas the had right "to establish an independent government" as long as the federal system had been disrupted and the nation was under a "reign of despotism." The resolution passed by a vote of thirty-three to fourteen.[2] It was intended to gain support both in the United States and Mexico. The Peace Party was forced to make the concession because a number of its delegates, including Austin, were still with the Army of the People outside Béxar. Thus, Austin's influence was considerably diminished by his and his supporters' absence from the meeting at San Felipe on this and other measures.

The delegates at the Consultation, urged on by the current emergency, established a military, the rules for which were made public on November 13, 1835.

Article 1: There shall be a regular army created for the protection of Texas during the recent war.

Art. 2: The regular army of Texas shall consist of one major general, who shall be commander in chief of all the forces called into public service during the war.

Art. 3: The commander-in-chief of the regular army of Texas shall be appointed by the convention and commissioned by the governor.

Art. 4: He shall be subject to the orders of the governor and council.

Art. 5: His staff shall consist of one adjutant general, one inspector general, one quartermaster general, one paymaster general, one surgeon general, and four aids-de-camp, with their respective ranks as in the United States army, in time of war to be appointed by the major general and commissioned by the governor.

Art. 6: The regular army of Texas shall consist of men enlisted for two years, and volunteers for and during the continuation of the war.

Art. 7: The regular army of Texas, while in service, shall be governed by the rules, regulations and discipline in all respects applicable to the regular army of the United States, in time of war, so far as is applicable to our condition and circumstances.

Art. 8: The regular army of Texas shall consist of eleven hundred and twenty men, rank and file.

Art. 9: There shall be a corps of rangers under the command of a major, to consist of one hundred and fifty men, to be divided into three or more detachments, and which shall compose a battalion under the commander-in-chief, when in the field.

Art. 10: The militia of Texas shall be organized as follows: all able bodied men, over sixteen, and under fifty years of age, shall be subject to militia duty.

Art. 11: Every inhabitant of Texas coming within purview of the preceding article shall, on the third Monday of December next, or as soon thereafter as practicable, assemble at each precinct of their municipality, and proceed to elect one captain, one first lieutenant, and one second lieutenant, to every fifty-six men.

Art. 12: When said elections shall have taken place, the judges shall certify to the governor forthwith, the names of the respective officers elected, who shall as soon as practicable make out and sign, and transmit commissions for the same; that if there shall be found to exist in any municipality, more than three companies, the captains or commandants, on giving due notice thereof, shall call together the subalterns of said companies and proceed to elect one major, if of four companies; one lieutenant colonel, if of five or more companies; one colonel for the command of said companies, which shall constitute a regiment in said municipality, the whole number of field and company officers shall, on due notice, proceed to elect a brigadier general out of their number, who shall command the whole militia in the said municipality.[3]

The Consultation had created the framework for a military force but it would not spring up overnight. Time and money were needed, and both were in short supply.

The Consultation also produced a framework for a civil government to oversee the revolution. Henry Smith was elected governor of the provisional government. The delegates also created a General Council to assist Smith. Born in the rush of the moment, the duties of the governor were not clearly defined, something that would have serious implications for Texas's military forces.[4]

On November 12, the delegates elected Sam Houston as "major general of the armies of Texas" and charged him not only to command the force but to raise it as well. It might be assumed with his election as commander "of the armies of Texas" that Houston could take charge of the Army of the People under Austin, but the democratic fervor of the era prevented it.[5] The same body that elected him major general denied him the use of that force, explaining that it would be unfair to make the volunteers "submit to the control of the provisional government" since they had been raised and its officers elected by their men before the Consultation met.[6] Houston found himself a general without an army.

The Consultation also had a position for Austin. On November 12, his friends offered him as a candidate to head the provisional government, but he lost to Henry Smith by a vote of thirty-one to twenty-two.[7] Later that day Austin's supporters nominated him as one of the agents authorized to travel to the "United States of North America" to promote Texas's cause. Austin was selected a commissioner along with Branch T. Archer and William H. Wharton. His election brought an end to his command of the Army of the People.

Austin had been ready to step down for some time, according to Houston. The former Tennessee governor had been one of the delegates who left Gonzales to visit the army outside Béxar. Austin invited him to drill the troops, which he did until he aroused the jealously of some in camp who had designs on higher office. Austin welcomed his presence, he said, and even asked him to take command of the troops, saying that Houston's recent election as Commander-in-Chief of the Department of Nacogdoches gave him authority to take over the responsibility. Houston declined, saying that the men had elected Austin and this assumption of command would disappoint the troops and cause discontent. Thus, Houston left the army in Austin's hands and journeyed to San Felipe where he took his seat as a delegate at the Consultation.[8]

Historians have generally not considered Austin a true military leader. An examination of his record, however, reveals him to have been well-versed in military matters. He had served in the Missouri militia during a short campaign in 1813 as regimental quartermaster. He had received a commission as lieutenant colonel in the Mexican militia in 1824 as part of his responsibility for serving as *empresario* for his colony. Acting on this authority, he proceeded to organize his colonists into a five-company battalion. Prior to his ill-fated mission to Mexico City, Austin actively oversaw military expeditions against tribes that harassed his colonists, in person and through his written orders. Austin called out his colony's militia to support the Mexican government during the 1826 Fredonia Rebellion. The colonists, by electing Austin commander of the Army of the People in 1835, had not just chosen a popular leader—they were electing someone experienced in working with volunteers. Austin's election should be viewed as part of the tradition of civic leaders like Andrew Jackson who were called on to serve in the field when needed. An educated man, Austin had made it a point to learn about military matters as expected of a republican leader of his station. It is interesting to think how events may have turned out if Austin had been retained in some political or military capacity instead of being sent to the United States at this critical time in the revolution.

Once appointed major general, Houston quickly began to express his views on how the war should be conducted. Although he had no authority over the volunteers before Béxar, he began corresponding with acquaintances serving there. On November 13, the day after his election as major general, he wrote to James W. Fannin to offer him the position of inspector general of the Texas Army. He expressed his views to Fannin, asking the former West Point cadet

> Wou'd it be best to raise a *nominal siege*:—fall back to Labehia and Gonzales, leaving a sufficient force for the protection of the frontier (which by the bye, will not be invaded) furlough the balance of the army to comfortable homes, and when the Artillery, is in readiness, march to the combat with sufficient force and at once reduce San Antonio!

He closed his message by saying, "Remember one Maxim, it is better to do well, *late*; than *never!* The army without means should have never passed the Guadalupe without the proper munitions of war to reduce San Antonio.—Therefore the error cannot be in falling back to an eligible position." Even at this early date, Houston expressed his opposition to military operations at Béxar.[9]

Houston believed the main body of the army should be quartered at Gonzales. He wrote Wylie Martin on November 24 that "it shall be proper or even necessary for the army of the people before Béxar to fall back." In his opinion, Gonzales was "the most important interior key to Texas (proper)" and it should be "placed in a condition for defence, with a force of from one to two hundred placed there, under a firm and prudent commander, who will at once establish discipline and organization; and using the greatest vigilance, retaining a few horses to keep out scouts. This, it seems to me, must be a rallying point for Texas."[10] Béxar never had the allure for Houston that it did for others, as evidenced by his words to an acquaintance: "It is probable that San Antonio will soon fall; but if she does not for the present, it is not important to Texas."[11]

Houston may have resented the fact that he had no authority over those troops already in the field. Nevertheless, he went about the business of creating his army from literally nothing. He estimated that Texas needed five thousand men to counter the ten thousand troops that it was falsely rumored Santa Anna had ordered to Texas. On December 4, Houston urged the new government to act on military matters at once, saying, "So soon as the army is organized by the Council, I will delay no time in raising an army to meet the Enemy on the earliest day possible." He warned that "Munitions for War with provisions and supplies for the army to be organized are not yet contracted for."[12] Two days later, he asked Governor Smith to urge the General Council to grant the commissions that would create his officer corps. He exclaimed to the governor, "An army has never been raised for Regular service until the officers had all been appointed. The regiments of the U. States army were all completely officered before one man was enlisted in the ranks."[13] Houston contended that he could not raise his army until he had a full complement of officers to oversee recruiting and training needed to build and disciple it. From the General Council, Houston request that they allow him to add a "General Judge advocate" to his staff, explaining that "In the Army every thing to be executed well must be executed promptly. Hence the *necessity* of a Gentleman who, can instantly respond to the Generals requirements on subjects to which his investigations cannot be extended, without embarrassment to his other duties."[14]

The General Council, somewhat irked by Houston's insinuation that it was somehow remiss in its duty, responded nevertheless with a series of actions designed to give Texas an effective military force. On November 21, the Committee on Military Affairs recommended appointing "at least one half of the officers immediately, from the Captains on down, in order that when reported for duty, to the Commander in Chief, they may be ordered on recruiting service: a measure which they deem essentially necessary to filling up the ranks of the regular army."[15] On November 28, the General Council nominated and appointed the company officers to staff the regular infantry regiment to be raised by Houston. It also nominated and appointed the officers for three companies that were to compose a Corps of Rangers. The council postponed electing the field officers of the infantry regiment but chose Robert M. Williamson to serve as major in command of the rangers. Not every man offered a commission would accept it, but at least the General Council gave Houston officers with which he could begin recruiting his army.[16]

The General Council responded to Houston's complaints to the governor. The Military Committee reported to the council as a whole that "no impediment or obstacle [has been thrown] in the way of raising the regular army, for the protection of Texas during the present war." Their report went on to say that the situation was just the opposite, "the General Council has been as expeditious in the enactment of ordinances, the election of Officers, and every other necessary arrangement, in order to carry into full force and effect the first article of the organic law, to which our attention is called by the letter of General Sam Houston, as could be done under the press of business, and the distracted state of our affairs." Besides, Houston should realize that the council had to devote attention to the army of volunteers then operating outside of Béxar, too.

The Military Committee went on to explain why it had been reluctant to appoint all regular officers at one time. The war may go on for some time and Texas might have to rely on volunteers from the United States. The members of the General Council recognized that "Texas now presents a fine field for those who desire military fame." They reasoned that "Men of talent, wealth or influence, will never submit to become privates in a regular army." Holding back some commissions as incentive would "leave the door open for promotion, so that if any person should make application for an appointment in the regular army, who is well recommended, and can bring one or more companies to our assistance, should be promoted to some office."[17]

THE GOVERNOR AND GENERAL COUNCIL AT ODDS

On November 15, the General Council members took a step that complicated the military situation. They had determined not to issue commissions until they had communicated "with some of the most influential and active officers of the present army, now before Béxar, that their views and intentions may be distinctly understood." The move was apparently initiated to determine whether the volunteers should stay in place or withdraw to Gonzales, but it opened the door for intrigue and personal projects that interfered and even competed with the organization of the regular army. On December 4, letters from William B. Travis and Fannin arrived at San Felipe and were referred to the Military Committee. Fannin's correspondence, which had been addressed to Governor Smith, expressed his belief that the number of troops already authorized to defend Texas should be doubled. He recommended increasing the regular force by another brigade and appointing a brigadier general to command each brigade, something that would require the authorization of two more generals to the Texas military establishment. Fannin warned that it would take at least six months "of the strictest squad drill" to prepare soldiers for the field, let alone to train the officers needed to command the force. The council and others placed stock in Fannin's opinion on the military because he had attended West Point, although he did not graduate. He informed the governor that several officers of the United States Army—"Civil, Military and Top[ographica]l Engineers"—had already tendered their service to him. As early as August he had contacted Francis M. Belton, a major in the U.S. Army stationed at Mobile, Alabama, enlisting his help to promote service in Texas among that nation's officer corps. He suggested that an "Agent selected by [the governor] & furnished with the requisite blank Commissions and other instructions, can in a few weeks, have a Brigade thus officered (at least from the rank of Captain to that of Coln) recruited as Emigrants in the U States, by the several officers themselves, and ready to take to the field, whenever the enemy invades our Territory."[18] The simplicity of the plan was that the brightest officers from the United States Army, if properly induced and rewarded, would recruit and organize the second brigade Fannin claimed was needed to defend Texas.

Fannin had evidently discussed his ideas with Travis. While admitting his own limited military experience, Travis told the governor and council, "I approve cherfully the views & reasoning on the subject of the Regular Army, expressed in the Communication of Capt. J. W. Fannin jr." Having endorsed Fannin's plan, Travis went on to state that he believed a brigade of volunteers should be authorized because it would take time for the regular army to be organized. He also suggested that a cavalry battalion should be authorized, as this branch had been overlooked in the creation of Texas's military establishment, but that such a corps was essential. "You must have well organized cavalry, before your armies will ever move quickly— That the arms of the cavalry should be broadswords, pistols & double barrelled shot guns or yaegers," he told them. The volunteer corps "should be mustered for twelve months unless the war should sooner be brought to a close and should be subject to regular discipline & the 'rules & articles' of War." He warned, "A mob can do wonders in a sudden burst of patriotism or of passion, but cannot be depended on, as soldiers for a campaign."[19]

The General Council, impressed with Fannin's argument and Travis's endorsement, quickly took the matter under consideration. Both men had expressed the need for an additional brigade. When faced with the choice of authorizing additional regulars or accepting the service of volunteers, the council chose "citizen-soldiers." Thus, on December 5, it created a Corps of Permanent Volunteers. The action mirrored a practice that had been used by the United States Congress when it authorized the creation of volunteer regiments to augment the regular military establishment during the War of 1812.

The creation of an auxiliary corps, although it seemed expedient, actually generated confusion. The regular army, on which the future defense of the nation rested, barely existed except on paper. Volunteers serving in the field refused to recognize Houston's authority, acting with little direction or allegiance to anyone. Men saw no reason to join the regular army, which Americans believed was a demeaning service for republicans such as themselves, when they could join the volunteer corps. The plum of high military office held out by the creation of a brigade also caused dissension among those who hoped to command it.

To make matters worse, the civil government established by the rebels collapsed when Governor Henry Smith and the General Council entered into a personal feud with disastrous results for Texas. Smith had little faith in a restored Mexican Federal Republic or the ability of Mexican Federalists to be faithful allies to the Texans. Acting in support of the Declaration of Causes designed to promote cooperation between Texas and other opponents to Centralism, the General Council authorized aid for Mexican Federalists Mexía and Gonzales. Smith refused to sign the measure and told the council, "I consider it bad policy to fit out, or trust Mexicans in any manner connected with our government, as I am well satisfied that we will in the end find them inimical [e.g. hostile] and treacherous."[20] He also informed Burleson at Béxar that "the Council contrary to my Knowledge or Consent furnished to Colo. Gonzales an outfit of $500 to cooperate with you to the reduction of that place." He cautioned, "I have no faith in him And you will keep a strict eye on him." The governor even went so far as to authorize Burleson, if he saw fit, to arrest Gonzales and his men and detain them as prisoners of war subject to Smith's orders.[21] The governor's attitude hampered the council's effort to build a working relationship with Mexican Federalists.

Smith also clashed with the council on another important matter that grew out of the desire to support Mexican Federalists. A plan had arisen for Texas to aid the larger Federalist cause by mounting a military campaign that would broaden the front. Reports from the interior indicated that other Mexican states were on the verge of revolt and only needed a show of support from Texas in order to proclaim against Santa Anna. The idea was to send an expedition to Matamoros. The proposed Matamoros Expedition found support among members of the General Council. Writing on December 25, the military committee recommended the project, citing its many benefits: (1) idle troops should be put to work or they would cause trouble, (2) the capture of Matamoros would keep it out of the hands of the Centralists and thus deny them a staging ground for an attack on Texas, (3) control of Matamoros, a port city, would provide revenue that could help fund the revolt in Texas, (4) troops and supplies could be landed to mount a southern campaign, (5) control of Matamoros would give the Texans command of the Gulf of Mexico eastward to New Orleans. Moreover, the expedition would support a Federalist uprising in surrounding areas. Thus, the Matamoros Expedition seemed to provide a new direction to the revolt now that Béxar had been captured.[22]

The governor initially supported the idea. On December 17, Smith instructed Houston to "adopt such Measures as you may deem best, for the reduction of Matamoros—and the occupation of such posts you may deem necessary for the protection of the frontier."[23] That same day Houston wrote to James Bowie, telling him "In obedience to the order of his excellency Henry Smith, Governor of Texas, of this date, I have the honor to direct that, in the event you can obtain the services of a sufficient number of men for the purpose, you will forthwith proceed on the route to Matamoros, and if possible reduce the place and retain possession until further notice." Should this not be possible, Bowie was to harass the enemy "conformably to the rules of civilized warfare." "Much is referred to your discretion," Houston told Bowie.[24] The problem for Smith and Houston was that Bowie did not receive the message for several weeks, delaying the project and giving the impression to the General Council that the governor and the general were not serious about carrying it out.

The General Council members decided to take matters into their own hands. They had intended to give the mission to Mexía, who had offered his services to Texas in the wake of the Tampico episode, but worsening relations with the Mexican Federalists caused them to reconsider. They also passed over Philip Dimitt, commander of Goliad, who had promoted the expedition. On December 15, the council wrote to Edward Burleson at Béxar proposing he oversee an expedition against Matamoros employing some of the volunteers under his command. The council was unaware that Burleson had written Smith that he was quitting the field and leaving Béxar. Burleson had informed the governor he was placing "the garrison and town under the command of colonel Johnson, with a sufficient number of men and officers to sustain the same, in case of attack, until assisted from the colonies; so that your Excellency may consider our conquest as sufficiently secured against every attempt of the enemy. The rest of the army will retire to their homes."[25] The council's instructions were received and opened by Frank W. Johnson. The project appealed to him and he replied on December 25 that "An expedition of this nature you point out has occupied our attention for some time."[26] On January 3, 1836, Johnson, who had traveled to San Felipe, informed the council members by note that he had opened the letter addressed to Burleson and had acted on it, initiating the expedition they had suggested. He told them that "the Volunteers left Béxar on the 30th of December last for Labahia and from thence to the destined point."[27] He also informed them, "I have left in garrison at Béxar 100 men under Command of Lieut Col Neill. This force I consider to be barely sufficient to hold the post and it will require at least Fifty additional troops to place it in a strong defensive position. I have ordered all the guns from the town into the alamo and the fortifications in the town to be destroyed."[28]

After reading this note, the council voted to give Johnson command of the expedition later that same day. On January 6, Johnson declined the appointment in a dispute with the council over status of the volunteers then under his command. The following day, however, he wrote the council, "I am content to bury in my own bosom all cause of complaint," further saying, "I shall proceed in the contemplated expedition and do all I can for the safety and protection of Texas."[29]

In the meantime, the General Council believed that Johnson had withdrawn his name from consideration and appointed Fannin to command the expedition in his place. The council did not revoke Johnson's commission, meaning that both he and Fannin had authority to raise volunteers and proceed to Matamoros. Although Smith, Houston, and Bowie eventually withdrew their support from

the project, the expedition at one point actually had three commanders: Bowie, Johnson, and Fannin. Texas sank into disorder and
discord as eyes turned toward Matamoros. Divided, Texas was
unprepared for the Centralist counterattack.

Chapter Five
Defending Béxar

The salvation of Texas depends in great measure in keeping Bejar out of the hands of the enemy. It serves as a frontier picquet guard and if it were in the possession of Santa Anna there is no strong hold from which to repell him in his march towards the Sabine.[1]

James Bowie
February 2, 1836

The sleeping garrison savored its last moments of rest. Soon the sun would rise and Santa Anna's cannon would again open fire on the old mission. The guns had been oddly silent through the night, allowing the tired men to slumber. They welcomed the quiet, safe in the knowledge that their pickets were in place to warn them in case of an attack. It was possible, however, that some of the pickets were also lulled to sleep. Volunteers did not adhere to the strict discipline of the regulars that imposed the death sentence on any soldier found asleep at his post during wartime. Such a doctrine was considered unsuited for free-born men.

Many of the *soldados* found the cold and tension prevented sleep from finding them. The hours they had spent on the damp ground allowed a chill to seep deep into their bodies. The strain wore on nerves. When would it start? Someone could stand the wait no longer and cried out into the dawn, "Viva La Republica!" Other picked up his *grito* and added "Viva Santa Anna!" The general was angered that his orders had been disobeyed. Surely the shouting would alert the garrison and cost him the element of surprise. He had to act quickly to preserve the momentum of the attack. His buglers broadcast his decision for the assault to begin without further wait. Santa Anna's *soldados* arose and marched en masse toward the Alamo as rockets lit the sky.

The Town and Its People

Béxar was already 118 years old in 1836. The town, which occupied the inside of a loop made by the meandering San Antonio River, began as a collection of religious, civil, and military communities, each with a specific purpose. The first of these to be established was Mission San Antonio de Valero, founded on the west bank of the river on May 5, 1718. Just four days later, Spanish officials also established a military settlement called Presidio San Antonio de Béxar. That same day Spanish officials laid out the boundary of a civil community, to be called La Villa de Béxar, just west of the newly founded fort. The civil town failed to develop because settlers from Mexico's interior could not be enticed to the frontier. In 1731, Spanish officials imported fifteen families from the Canary Islands to provide the basis of a population for a new town, San Fernando de Béxar. Mission San Antonio had two temporary locations along the river before being relocated on the east bank in 1724, opposite the bend in which the presidio and town were founded. Later an unofficial community sprang up south of Mission San Antonio called La Villita or the little town. Although initially separate entities, their respective residents knew each other well. Captain William Carey, whose company of volunteer artillery was stationed at the Alamo, described the town and its old mission to his family: "The town has two Squares in it and the church the centre, one a military and the other a government square. The Alamo or the fort as we call it, is a very old building, built for the purpose of protecting the citizens from hostile Indians."[2]

Béxar served as the governmental seat for Texas throughout its Spanish tenure. The military commander at the presidio often served as governor of the province. Béxar lost its position as capital when the Federal Constitution of 1824 attached Texas to Coahuila. Nevertheless, the town remained the governmental seat for the Department of Béxar and preserved its standing as an important place. In May 1835, Governor José Maria Viesca had designated Béxar the state capital but it never actually served as the working capital of Coahuila y Tejas.

The local government of Béxar was well established by the 1830s. Town government under the Spanish system consisted of an *alcalde* (a position that combined the duties of mayor and municipal judge) and *ayuntamiento* (city council). The town itself had been divided into four districts, each with its own *regidore* (alderman): Barrio Valero encompassed the communities of former Mission San Antonio and La Villita; Barrio del Sur took in the area south of the military and civil plazas; Barrios del Norte covered the area north of the military and civil plazas; and Barrio de Laredo represented the sparse settlement west of San Pedro Creek on the edge of the town. The *ayuntamiento* passed ordinances that regulated commerce, ensured public safety, and other important public matters.[3]

The military and civil plazas formed the center of the town. Around these lived some of the town's most prominent citizens. The plazas were also the location of civil, military, and religious activity. San Fernando Church dominated Béxar from its position on the western side of the civil plaza, providing a visual focal point for the community. The main east-west street passing through the town was called Calle del Portero, also known as the Alameda because its eastern end was lined with cottonwood trees. (The modern name of this avenue is Commerce Street.)

The town reflected the distinctive architecture of the region. The more substantial houses were single-story rectangular structures with flat roofs, whose rooms opened onto a central courtyard. The exteriors of these houses had an entryway that could be closed by heavy wooden doors. Windows facing out onto the street were usually small and lacked glass panes. The fortress-like appearance of these homes was no accident as the design provided protection in case of attack. The interior of these houses was traditionally sparsely furnished, with a table, a few chairs or benches, and hooks or shelves for kitchenware. Beds were sometimes built into the walls, providing a low couch on which blankets or hides could be spread. Floors were packed earth. A fireplace occupied a corner with a hole cut in the roof above to allow the smoke to exit. An earthen oven for baking breads and roasting meats could be found in the courtyard. Walls were plastered, whitewashed, and decorated to make rooms more appealing to their occupants. Roofs were flat, made of timbers laid flat and placed side to side on which a thick layer of earth was piled to form a mostly waterproof barrier.

Another type of house, the *jacale*, could also be found in Béxar. *Jacales* were small houses (often just one room) made by driving tall wooden stakes into the ground to form a stockade-like structure. The floor was earth and the roof was thatch. A fire-pit provided heat and light. Béxar's poorer residents lived in this style of housing. Crude but comfortable, *jacales* were a common feature throughout Mexico.

The San Antonio River provided the lifeblood of Béxar. The Spaniards had chosen to locate their settlements in the area because of the nearby springs that gave rise to the river and creeks. One nineteenth century observer claimed the river at Béxar ran about six feet deep and was crystal clear, allowing a view of the rounded rocks that lined its bottom and the fish that swam through its currents. Because it was built next to the river, Béxar was subject to flooding some years, as in 1819 when nearly fifty buildings were damaged or destroyed. A bridge over the river on Calle del Portero and a ford across from La Villita connected the two sides of the community. During the Spanish rule, *acequias* or irrigation ditches had been built that led from the river, providing the town and the areas' missions with water and making it possible to grow crops in an otherwise dry region. The river flowed southward from Béxar, running by the four other missions located there by the Spanish. Nearly seventy miles downstream lay Presidio La Bahía and the town of Goliad. From there the river continued on to the Gulf of Mexico. Cópano, located near the river's mouth, served a landing for goods arriving by ship, most often illegally.

Béxar lay on one of the main routes through Texas, connecting Saltillo to the Nacogdoches-San Augustine region that lay along the Texas-Louisiana border. The road leading into Béxar from the west brought travelers and goods from the Rio Grande towns of Presidio Del Rio Grande and Laredo. Travelers going east from Béxar had the choice of heading northeast to Nacogdoches, east to Gonzales, or southeast to Goliad. Besides the official byways, a myriad of trails led in and out of Béxar, many used by smugglers who brought contraband to sell to the town's residents.

Although an 1831 census placed Béxar's population at only 1,634, the town was estimated to have grown to 2,000 by 1836.[4] Many of the more influential residents had a home in town as well as a ranch outside the city. Ethnically, Béxareños were a mixture of the people who had been brought to settle the area and the native population that they had found living along the river. Many Spanish soldiers had married mission residents and their progeny made up a significant portion of the population. The Canary Islanders (who had been granted titles and rights of nobility as an incentive for settling in Texas) tried to maintain their pure Spanish bloodlines but found it increasingly difficult in a frontier community like Béxar. Many Indians who had adopted Spanish customs and lifestyle lived on the edge of town, somewhat symbolizing their relationship with Béxar's elite. Although some Americans had made their way to Béxar prior to the opening of Texas to colonists, most were imprisoned by Spanish authorities, who discouraged intercourse between the two countries.

Nevertheless, visitors to Béxar were starting to notice differences between it and other Mexican towns. A Swiss botanist, Jean Louis Berlandier, passed through the town in 1828 as a member of the Mexican Boundary Commission. He wrote, "Trade with the Anglo-Americans, and the blending in to some degree of their customs, make the inhabitants of Texas a little different from the Mexicans of the interior, whom those in Texas call foreigners and whom they scarcely like." Berlandier attributed Tejanos' dislike of people from the interior to the fact that those closer to Mexico City believed themselves superior to their countrymen on the frontier. He further highlighted the connection between the United States and Béxar, saying, "the women prefer to dress in the fashion of Louisiana, and by doing so they participate both in the customs of the neighboring nation and of their own." He and others criticized the residents' seeming lack of interest in improving the agricultural productive as they seemed satisfied to plant only enough beans, corn, squash and peppers needed for survival. Not only did this practice fail to consider the potential loss of crops to bad weather, it also meant that there was no surplus to sell and thereby improve the town's economy. Berlandier blamed the military ties to the community, which he said promoted indolence. Critics like Berlandier pointed to the Americans, whose settlements flourished, as examples of what could be accomplished in Texas with effort.[5]

For many Mexican observers, the American settlements were not only an example of the bounty Texas offered, they were a cause of concern. While the 1831 census showed Béxar's population numbered 1,634, the much younger town of San Felipe de Austin boasted a population of 5,665. Both communities listed agriculture as the primary occupation of its heads of household. San Felipe, however, had three categories of workers not found in Béxar: lawyer, printer, and slave. Thus, some fundamental differences remained between the Bexareños and the Anglos as all three occupations played important roles in helping to make the American political and economic systems of that time such a dynamic force.

The Effects of Revolutionary Politics on the Béxar Garrison

Béxar's strategic location, economic importance, and political significance dictated that it must be controlled. The colonists had recognized this fact as early as the summer of 1835. Santa Anna had sent Cos to reinforce Ugartechea and had additionally directed General Joaquín Ramírez y Sesma to march to Cos's relief when he learned that Béxar was besieged by the rebels. For the insurgents, control of Béxar indicated that the revolt was succeeding; for the Centralists, control of Béxar demonstrated that the government had re-exerted its authority over the town and surrounding area. Thus, it was a prize worth fighting for and could not be abandoned by the rebels or bypassed by the Centralists.

The battle of Béxar had firmly placed the town in the hands of the rebels for the time being. Although many of the colonists had returned home, more than four hundred volunteers remained throughout most of December. These were the remnants of the Army of the People that had been inherited by Burleson after Austin had been called away. Burleson departed shortly after the rebel victory and command of the army fell to his former aide, Frank W. Johnson. The Matamoros Expedition, which was then under discussion, seriously hampered the rebels' ability to defended Béxar should the Centralists return.

Houston had begun making plans for the defense of Texas and the disposition of troops that would be required. On December 15, Houston wrote to a member of the General Council detailing what actions were needed prior to the commencement of the spring campaign, exclaiming "I propose placing a field officer in command of San Antonio de Béxar with a sufficient number of Troops for the defence of the station." He also planned to employ "an engineer, and [to] have the fortifications and defences of the place improved." La Bahía, too, must also be occupied with a force of fifty to one hundred men under the command of a competent officer. Additionally, he concluded that the landing at Cópano had to be protected by controlling either Refugio or San Patricio.[6] With these places secured, Texas could go about the business of gathering supplies and organizing its army. Houston made the proposal unaware that Matamoros fever was about to sweep across Texas.

Within a week, Houston was acting on his proposed plan. On December 20, Houston directed James W. Fannin, the newly appointed colonel of the 1st Regiment of Texas Artillery, to proceed to Matagorda, where he was to establish his headquarters to begin enlisting and training recruits.[7] The following day, Houston sent instructions to Béxar for James C. Neill, the officer second-in-command of Fannin's regiment. Neill had been recommended for a post in the regular artillery by his neighbor D.C. Barrett, who contended that "age and experience with his militia rank & title, would seem to justify his first commission as a field officer."[8] Houston instructed Neill that "On receipt of this you will take command of the Post of Béxar and make such disposition of the troops there as you may deem proper for the security & protection of the place." He asked that a report detailing the state of the defenses along with a complete inventory of what was on hand as well as what was needed be sent to him as soon as possible. He specifically directed that Green B. Jameson assist in this task. He further instructed Neill to "detail some capable officer to assist in fortifying the place in the best manner possible." In closing, Houston stated that "The Commander in Chief in depositing the high trust of the command of Béxar to Col. J.C. Neill feels assured that the confidence is not misplaced & that he will always be able to respond to the country in defence of its rights."[9] Writing on December 26, Houston mused, "Today there has been an arrival in six days from San Antonio, which reports all quiet, but no discipline. Ere this I hope my order has reached them, and will have the proper effect with the command."[10]

Houston's hope for calm and order in Béxar evaporated with the arrival of news from Neill. On January 6, the government received a letter from the post's commander that detailed the situation that existed there. Wrote Neill, "It will be appalling to you to learn and see herewith enclosed our alarming weakness. . . . We have 104 men and two distinct fortresses to garrison, and about twenty-four pieces of artillery." The source of their problem, he continued, was that Frank W. Johnson and Dr. James Grant, aide-de-camp to General Burleson, had confiscated clothing and provisions intended to see the garrison through the winter for their own use in the march on Matamoros. He complained, "If a divide had been made of them, the most needy of my men could have been made comfortable by the stocks of clothing and provisions taken from here." In addition to taking supplies, Johnson and Grant, had enticed nearly two hundred men who had volunteered to garrison Béxar to go with them, violating the terms of their enlistment. He estimated that at least two hundred men were required to man the post at all times with perhaps an additional one hundred required to help complete the fortifications necessary to defend Béxar.[11]

Neill's report widened the rift that had developed between the governor and the council. Houston forwarded it to Smith the same day he received it and requested that the governor "render to the cause of Texas and humanity" and refer it "to the general council of the provisional government, in secret session." The general placed the problem in Smith's hands, writing that he was going to Goliad to survey the situation there created by the council's attempt to raise a force for the Matamoros Expedition.[12] Houston still had not left on January 8 when he wrote Smith that he would set out in less than an hour's time for the army, where he would do all he could to stop the headlong rush to the Rio Grande. He believed that the plan was not only ill-conceived, it was illegal, too, writing "I am told that Frank Johnson and Fannin have obtained from the Military Committee orders to Proceed and reduce Matamoras. It may not be so. There was no Quorum, and the Council could not give power."[13]

The following day Smith submitted a letter to the General Council that ultimately left Texas with two competing civil governments. He began by saying "I herewith transmit to your body, the returns and correspondence of Colonel Neill, Lieutenant Colonel Commandant of the post at Béxar. You will in that correspondence find the situation of that Garrison." His tone was that of a father scolding disobedient children. He accused them of outfitting a piratical expedition and appointing their own "Generalissimo" to its command. Smith told the council members that, like them, he had been placed on a "political watchtower." The difference was, however, he was not willing to sacrifice the country to "the shrine of plunder." Smith warned "that after twelve o'clock to-morrow all communications between the two departments shall cease; and your body will stand adjourned until the first of March" unless the General Council publicly renounced its current course of action.[14]

The General Council resented Smith's accusations and denied he had the authority to order its dismissal. It issued a public proclamation, but not one Smith expected. The Matamoros Expedition, it contended, had been thought a good idea by the governor, who had backed the plan under the leadership of Houston's man, James Bowie. As for the current situation on the frontier, the council laid

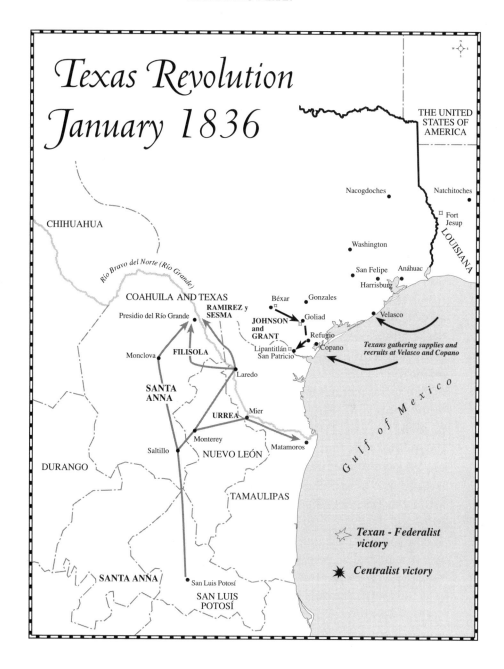

Texas Revolution
January 1836

THE UNITED
STATES OF
AMERICA

Nacogdoches
Natchitoches

Fort
Jesup

CHIHUAHUA

LOUISIANA

Washington

Río Bravo del Norte (Río Grande)

San Felipe   Anáhuac

Harrisburg

COAHUILA AND TEXAS

Béxar   Gonzales

RAMIREZ y
SESMA

Presidio del Río Grande

JOHNSON
and
GRANT

Goliad

Velasco

FILISOLA

Refugio

Monclova

Copano

Lipantitlán
San Patricio

*Texans gathering supplies and
recruits at Velasco and Copano*

Laredo

SANTA
ANNA

Mier

URREA

Monterey

Gulf of Mexico

Saltillo

NUEVO LEÓN

Matamoros

DURANGO

TAMAULIPAS

Texan - Federalist
victory

SANTA ANNA

San Luis Potosí

Centralist victory

SAN LUIS
POTOSÍ

the blame on the governor, explaining that General Burleson's aide-de-camp, Dr. James Grant, had put the expedition in action. The council denied ever granting the doctor any authority and claimed he must have been acting on behalf of the governor.[15] Having blamed the governor for all the confusion created at Béxar, the General Council declared his office vacant since he had chosen to cut off communication with them. Lieutenant Governor James Robinson was elected by the council as Smith's replacement. Not included in the council's proclamation, however, was the fact that its members knew that Bowie had been asked to lead the expedition and that they had muddied the issue by appointing two of their own men, Fannin and Johnson. There certainly was enough blame to go around but no one wanted to accept responsibility for the unfolding debacle.

Smith realized that he had overstepped his bounds and attempted a reconciliation with the council. Writing on January 12, he told the council "I admit that I [used] language beyond the rules of decorum" but he at the time felt that the council's actions were a direct insult to his office. He proclaimed that he was willing to forget the matter if the council admitted it had been wrong or convinced him that he had misunderstood its actions. If this could be accomplished, "the two branches [would] again harmonize to the promotion of the true interests of the country."[16] Informed that the gulf was too wide to bridge, Smith wrote the council that he cared "not for popularity" and that any consequence that came from standing against it was a sacrifice he willingly made "at the shrine of the public good."[17]

On January 14, 1836, Neill penned another letter to the governor and council that produced even more consternation. He wrote, "There can exist but little doubt that the enemy is advancing on this post, from the number of families leaving town today." Even John W. Smith, an American who had taken up residence in Béxar, had engaged a wagon to remove his family to the colonies. Neill had heard that a portion of the enemy had already advanced as far as the Rio Frio but was unable to verify the report due to the fact that the garrison lacked horses for a spy company. Only about seventy-five volunteers remained in Béxar to oppose the enemy's return and none of them had been paid since entering the service. Neill warned, "Unless we are reinforced and victualled, we must become an easy prey to the enemy, in case of an attack." He informed the government that, pending their response to his call, he had instructed his messenger to stop at Gonzales and ask the townspeople to forward as many horses and men as they could.[18]

Neill also addressed a letter to Houston on January 14, whom he had heard was on the march. He reiterated the woeful state of his command, saying that twenty of his men were leaving tomorrow, while "There are at Laredo now 3,000 men under command of General Ramirez, and two other generals, and, as it appears from a letter received last night, 1,000 of them are destined for this place, and two thousand for Matamoros." Neill defiantly exclaimed to his commander, "I hope that we will be re-inforced in eight days, or we will be overrun by the enemy, but, if I have only 100 men, I will fight 1,000 as long as I can and then not surrender."[19]

The message reached Houston at Goliad where he had gone to dissuade the volunteer army from carrying out its advance on Matamoros. He told the governor, "An express reached me from Lieutenant-Colonel Neill, of Béxar, of an expected attack from the enemy in force." Fearing the worst, Houston "immediately requested Colonel James Bowie to march with a detachment of volunteers to his relief [who] met the request with his usual promptitude and manliness."[20] Thus, Neill's plea for help yielded Bowie, one of the most dynamic personalities in Texas.

Houston forwarded Neill's letter to Smith and also informed him of a change in plans for the important rebel outpost. "Colonel Bowie will leave here in a few hours for Béxar with a detachment of from thirty to fifty men. Capt. Patton's Company, it is believed are now there." Believing that political squabbling, intrigue, and confusion had deprived the rebels of any chance of making a stand in the town, Houston decided to deny its use to the enemy and to salvage what he could of its military assets. "I have ordered the fortifications in the town of Béxar to be demolished, and, if you should think well of it, I will remove all the cannon and other munitions of war to

Gonzales and Copano, blow up the Alamo and abandon the place, as it will be impossible to keep up the Station with volunteers, the sooner I can be authorized the better it will be for the country."

Houston feared that his forward position might already be in jeopardy. He informed the governor that he had "sent to Capt. Demit to raise one hundred more men and march to Béxar forthwith, if it be invested; and if not to repair to headquarters with his company. Captain Patton will do likewise." The general wrote that he "would . . . have marched to Béxar [himself] but the Matamoras rage is up so high that [he] must see Colonel Ward's men."[21]

Houston's letter is telling because it contains important information about Béxar and its future defense. It places Bowie, one of the more notable figures in the upcoming siege, on the road to Béxar to assist Neill. The letter, morever, contends that Houston had provided for the town's temporary defense by ordering two additional companies there forthwith to cover that position while final dispositions of its cannons and stockpiles could be made. Thus, it appears at this point that Béxar was being reinforced although neither Dimitt nor Patton raised their respective companies as directed. Perhaps most importantly, though, the letter reveals that Houston no longer believed that the town should or could be defended.

Smith described the situation to the public in his January 22 address in which he defended his actions against the General Council. He exclaimed, "The siege of Bejar, with the consequences and subsequent management, I would suppose, ought to be sufficient to teach us a lesson. That fortress, the reduction of which has cost us so much, is now stripped, and left with only seventy naked men, destitute of clothing, provisions, ammunition, and every comfort, [and is now] threatened by a large invading Mexican army, who, hearing of the weakened situation of that garrison, had determined to re-take it."[22] Alerting the country to the precarious state of frontier defense, he made it clear that the blame for the approaching disaster lay with the General Council. Thus, the fate of Béxar had become embroiled in the feud between the governor and the council.

On January 23, Neill sent another letter from Béxar to the governor that fueled the Texians' anxiety while blurring the strategic situation. He wrote that Santa Anna was on his way to Texas with an army of ten thousand men "to reduce the State [to what] it originally was in 1820." He explained that Santa Anna intended "to attack Copano and Labahia first and send but a few hundred cavalry against this place at the same time." Neill had little doubt of the report's veracity, saying, "The foregoing information is received thr'u such a channel that the most implicit reliance may be given to its correctness and veracity, as the parties are personally Known to Coln Buoy [Bowie] and he says deserving the utmost confidence." Although Béxar was ultimately attacked by more than just a few hundred cavalry, the report correctly described the Centralist plan for the two-pronged campaign that was taking shape to smash the Texas rebels.

The letter further indicated that Bowie had arrived in Béxar as instructed by Houston. Neill addressed Houston's proposal to remove the artillery from town and to "blow up the Alamo and abandon the place." The problem with complying with such an order was connected to the actions of Johnson and Grant. Wrote Neill, "If teams could be obtained here by any means to remove the Cannon and Public Property I would immediately destroy the fortifications and abandon the place, taking the men I have under my command here, to join the Commander at Copanoe."[23] The garrison could withdraw but the artillery and public stores would have to be either destroyed or left for the enemy.

Smith, who did not agree with Houston's plan to abandon Béxar, had decided on his own to reinforce Neill and instead ordered him to remain in place. Travis had accepted a commission in the regular Texas Army as the lieutenant colonel in command of the newly authorized cavalry battalion he had suggested the council raise. The governor ordered him to collect what men he could and march to Béxar.

Neill, now taking his orders from the civilian leadership of rebel Texas rather than its appointed army commander, wrote the governor on January 28 regarding how he planned to use Travis's mounted force as an advance picket to spy and harass the approaching enemy. "I shall instruct Col. Travis to cut down the bridges over the Leona and Nueces to embarrass the enemy in crossing those streams," he wrote. "With the men, say 25, under that officer's command the force of this garrison will consist of 130 Americans and with 600 to 1000 men, I can oppose an effectual resistance."[24] Thus, Neill expected Travis's men to serve as an offensive buffer and trip wire between Béxar and the approaching Centralists.

Although Travis recognized Neill's need for mounted troops, he had problems of his own with which to contend before he could get his modest force underway. He wrote to Smith on January 28 to explain his situation. "In obedience to my orders, I have done every thing in my power to get ready to march to the relief of Béxar, but owing to the difficulty of getting horses and provisions, and owing to desertions, I shall march to-day with only about thirty men, all regulars except four."

Travis discerned that a trip to Béxar was hazardous at best, and his reaction was one of notable reluctance. He wrote, "I shall, however, go on and do my duty, if I am sacrificed. . . . Unless I receive new orders to countermarch." He cited a wide array of reasons for his slow start. "Our affairs are gloomy indeed. The people are cold and indifferent. They are worn down and exhausted with war, and, in consequences of dissentions between contending and rival chieftains, they have lost all confidence in their own government and officers." He, too, must have doubted the leadership of the rebellion. "Money must be raised or Texas is gone *to ruin*. Without it, war cannot be again carried on in Texas. The patriotism of a few has done much; but that is becoming worn down." Travis had already sacrificed much for the cause. "I have strained every nerve, I have used my personal credit, and have slept neither day nor night since I received orders to march, and, with all this, I have barely been able to get horses and equipments for the few men I have."[25]

Travis, having already sent that missive, penned another the following day to emphasize his reluctance for proceeding to Béxar. He held out hope that his small command would be spared being sent off to the frontier before they were ready. "I have been here with the troops under Capt. [John H.] Forsythe, but I shall await your orders at Gonzales, or some other point on the road. I shall, however, keep the thirty men of Forsythe's company in motion toward Béxar, so that they may arrive there as soon as possible."

He also expressed personal reasons for not wanting to go to Béxar. He argued that he was needed elsewhere, namely to recruit the balance of his battalion. "Not having been able to raise 100 volunteers agreeably to your orders, and there being so few regular troops together, I must beg that your Excellency will recall the order for me to go to Béxar in command of so few men." He asserted that he was not afraid of going, but gave the expedition very little chance for success. "I am willing, nay anxious, to go to the defence of Béxar, but, sir, I am unwilling to risk my reputation (which is ever dear to a soldier) by going off into the enemy's country with so little means, so few men, and with them so badly equipped." To cinch his argument, he observed that, with so few men on hand, a field grade officer would only confuse the issue. "In fact, there is no necessity for my services to command these few men," he wrote. "The company officers will be amply sufficient."[26] Smith did not yield to these arguments. As a result, Travis, the fiery young lawyer, did his duty and traveled on to Béxar with his meager command, arriving in the first week of February.

On February 2, Bowie, who had been in Béxar for almost two weeks, wrote Smith to update the governor of the overall strategic situation. First, he recounted his failed attempt to organize the proposed expedition to Matamoros. "In pursuance or your orders, I proceeded from San Felipe to La Bahia and whilst there employed my whole time in trying to effect the objects of my mission," he wrote. He also explained how the confusing chain of command amongst the rebel leadership had interrupted his exchanges with the governor. "You are aware that Genl Houston came to La Bahia soon after I did, this is the reason why I did not make a report to you from that post. The comdr. in chf. has before this communicated to you all matters in relation to our military affairs at La Bahia, this makes it wholly unnecessary for me to say any thing on the subject."

With that explained, Bowie then related how Neill's letter to Houston had prompted his change of orders and subsequent departure for Béxar. "Whilst at La Bahia Genl Houston received despatches from Col Comdt. Neill informing that good reasons were entertained that an attack would soon be made by a numerous Mexican

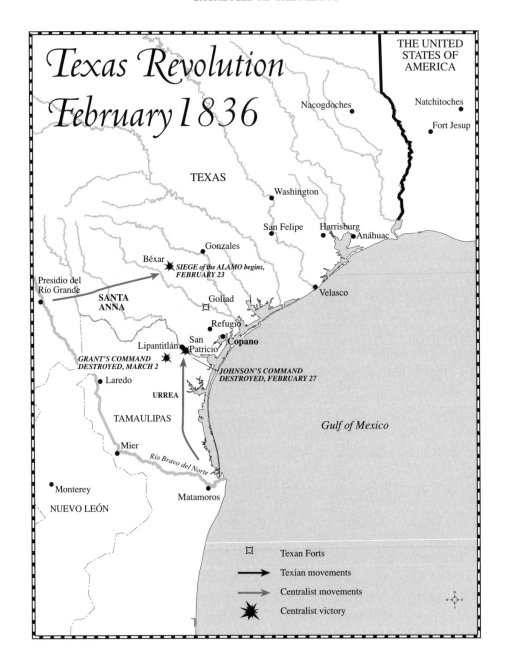

Army on our important post at Bejar," he wrote. "It was forthwith determined that I should go instantly to Bejar; accordingly I left Genl Houston and with very few efficient volunteers came to this place about two weeks since."

He then proceeded to describe what had happened at Béxar since his arrival and of his impressions of that post. "I was received by Col. Neill with great cordiality, and the men under my command entered at once into active service. All I can say of the soldiers stationed here is complimentary to both their courage and their patience."

Even so, the troops at the Alamo were suffering and morale was eroding. Bowie continued: "But it is the truth your Excellency must know it, that great and just dissatisfaction is felt for the want of a little money to pay the small but necessary expenses of our men." Even so, the garrison had persevered. "I cannot eulogise the conduct & character of Col. Neill too highly: no other man in the army could have kept men at this post, under the neglect they have experienced. Both he & myself have done all that we could; we have industriously tryed all expedients to raise funds; but hitherto it has been to no purpose. We are still laboring night and day, laying up provisions for a seige, encouraging our men, and calling on the Government for relief."

Having related how the garrison was endeavoring to maintain the post even though neglected by their government, Bowie turned his attention to pleading for assistance as he expected the Centralist advance at any time. "*Relief* at this post, in men, money, & provisions is of *vital importance* & and is wanted instantly. Sir, this is the object of my letter." Beyond the safety of his command, Bowie identified the strategic importance of their position. "The salvation of Texas depends in great measure in keeping Bejar out of the hands of the enemy. It serves as a frontier picquet guard and if it were in the possession of Santa Anna there is no strong hold from which to repell him in his march towards the Sabine." His spies and contacts reported that some two thousand Mexican soldiers were marshalling in towns across the Rio Grande. "Very large forces are being gathered ... with good officers, well armed, and a plenty provisions," he wrote, adding that they "were on the point of marching, (the provisions being cooked &c)."

Bowie also revealed that, although potentially dire, the object of this Mexican army's intentions remained unclear. "A detachment of active young men from the volunteers under my command have been sent out to the Rio Frio; they returned yesterday without information and we remain yet in doubt whether they entend an attack on this place or go to reinforce Matamoros," he wrote. Even so, he wanted to take no chances on his ability to hold Béxar, for sooner or later it would be attacked, and probably by troops moving up the road from Presidio del Rio Grande, and not from a coastal landing as had been earlier suggested. "It does . . . seem certain that an attack is shortly to be made on this place [and] that the enemy will come by land."

In conclusion, he pleaded for support, not only for his brave stalwarts, but also for his friends and neighbors. "The Citizens of Bejar have behaved well [and they] deserve our protection." That said, he also made clear that he would rather die there than abandon the place but also suggested that the enemy would soon learn of the wretched state of the garrison and would be quick to exploit it. "The public safety demands our lives rather than to evacuate this post to the enemy.—again we call aloud for *relief*; the weakness of our post will at any rate bring the enemy on." His attempts at summoning Smith's compassion only served to display how exposed Béxar really was. "Some volunteers are expected: Capt Patton with 5 or 6 has come in. But a large reinforcement with provisions is what we need. . . . Our force is very small, the returns this day the Comdt. Is only one hundred and twenty officers & men. It would be a waste of men to put our brave little band against thousands." Perhaps most significant of all, Bowie told Smith that "Col. Neill and Myself have come to the solemn resolution that we will rather die in these ditches than give it up to the enemy."[27]

Meanwhile, Neill had also written Smith about other matters beside reinforcements. On January 27, the commander of the post at Béxar informed the governor that his men had held a meeting three days earlier in which they determined to send their own delegates to the convention that was to begin on March 1 at Washington-on-the-Brazos. Municipalities had been choosing their representatives after word had gone out that the meeting was to be held. The citizens of Béxar had chosen four delegates: Antonio Navarro, José Francisco Ruiz, Erasmo Seguín, and Gaspar Flores. Nevertheless, the members of the garrison believed that they were entitled to elect their own delegates and proceeded to do so. A memorial address to the delegates who would soon gather on the banks of the Brazos River explained the garrison's reason for holding their own election. As many of the men were not citizens of Béxar, the general feeling was that they should not take part in the voting at that municipality. Moreover, many of the men were without a permanent residency and even those who had one would not have time to travel there in time to cast their ballots. The document explained that the garrison did not believe that the delegates from Béxar could represent them ". . . inasmuch as the members sent from this municipality though they have the best intentions, are yet unable, from the difference of language & habits, to represent the Anglo American and Army interest." Three captains serving at Béxar conducted the election that selected two men to represent the garrison: Samuel A. Maverick and Jesse B. Badgett, both of whom were recognized and seated when they arrived at Washington-on-the-Brazos.[28]

With such political business behind him and the case for holding Béxar at all cost strongly made, Neill turned again to military matters and set about to make the Alamo as defensible as possible. His chief architect for this defense was Green B. Jameson. On January 18, Jameson forwarded a detailed report to Houston describing the steps he had taken to make Alamo defensible. "I send you herewith inclosed a neat plot of the fortress exhibiting its true condition at this time," he wrote. He had made good use of the heavy guns on hand. "I am now fortifying and mounting the cannon. The 18 pounder now on the N.W. corner of the fortress so as to command the Town and the country around."

The garrison had begun new routines and was ever vigilant. "The officers of every department do more than the men and also stand guard, and to act as patrol every night." Even so, Jameson seemed certain that his plans had been compromised. "I have no doubt but the enemy have spies in town every twenty-four hours, and we are using our utmost endeavors to catch them every night, nor have I any doubt but there are 1500 of the enemy at the town of Rio Grande, and as many more at Laredo, and I believe they know our situation as well as we do ourselves."

The Alamo garrison had a decent stockpile of provisions, but more would be useful. "We have received 100 bushels of meal and 42 Beeves which will last us for two months yet to come, but no other supplies have come to our relief." If needed, food might be obtained from friends in town. "We can rely on aid from the citizens of this town in case of a siege, Saguine [Seguín] is doing all for the cause he can, as well as many of the most wealthy and influential citizens."

Jameson also described what to the defenders was plainly obvious. "You can plainly see by the plot that the Alamo never was built by a military people for a fortress, tho' it is strong, there is not a redoubt that will command the whole line of the fort." Even so, Jameson felt confident that with a few modifications—including finishing the half moon batteries—he could make a decent defense with the number of cannons on hand. Given a few months, he might have entirely redesigned the place, but being short of both time and workers, he would make due with what he had. "The men here will not labour and I cannot ask it of them until they are better clad and fed."

While the shortage of manpower, the physical condition of the troops, and their lack of training all pointed to a potential disaster, Jameson remained optimistic. "We now have 114 men counting officers, the sick and wounded which leaves us about 80 efficient men. 40 in the Alamo and 40 in Town, leaving all the patrole duty to be done by the officers and which for want of horses has to be performed on foot. We have had loose discipline untill lately." His plan was to withdraw the garrison of the town into his improvised citadel and there to make a stand 'In case of an attack we will move all into the Alamo and whip 10 to 1 with our artillery."

He further argued that with proper support, the small garrison would make a great showing in any future contest. "If the men here can get a reasonable supply of clothing, provisions and money they will . . . fight better than fresh men, they have all been tried and have confidence in themselves."

No matter what the future held, Jameson declared his intentions. "I can give you full assurance that so far as I am concerned there shall be nothing wanting on my part, neither as an officer or a soldier, to promote and sustain the great cause at which we are all aiming," he wrote. He was proud of his fort, and the men who watched from atop its walls. "I have been much flattered for my exertions at this place. I have than one time received the vote of thanks of the whole Garrison."

Jameson clearly believed that even with his rudimentary attempts to improve the place, it would withstand an enemy assault. He began to look to the future. "I will in my next [report] give you a plan of the Town as fortified when we took it. We have too few to garrison both places, and will bring all our forces to the Alamo tomorrow as well as the cannons." He wrote that the water supply of the fort was adequate, and he described plans for extensive earthworks. "We can ditch near the half moon batteries with perfect safety," he wrote. "I shall be able to show you by demonstration when I have nothing else to attend to that I will not be wanting in my abilities as a topographical engineer."[29] A lawyer by training, Jameson demonstrated in his letter to Houston that he grasped the main concepts concerning military engineering and that he eagerly accepted the challenge of placing the former mission compound in a defensible condition.

Jameson kept the governor and civilian leadership informed of his progress, too. Writing nearly a month later on February 11, he told Smith the defenses were not yet complete and his earlier enthusiasm had waned. "We are badly prepared to meet them. Though we will do the best we can." The lack of pay and provisions still rankled the garrison, Jameson contended, adding that "A great number of the volunteers will leave to morrow." To compensate for the dwindling number of men to defend the place, Jameson wrote, "I have some improved demonstrations to make & send you of our Fortress whereby fewer men and less Artillery will be required in case of a siege or attack."[30]

As promised, the Alamo's engineer sent the governor more details of his intended plan five days later, asking Smith for his opinion, hoping to receive permission to proceed with the work. His intentions were to totally rework the place after all. "The suggestion is, to square the Alamo and erect a large redoubt at each corner supported by Bastions & leave a ditch all around full of water. When squared in that way four cannon & fewer men would do more effective service than twenty of artillery does or can do in the way they are now mounted."[31] No record exists whether or not Smith approved Jameson's plan to restructure the old mission compound, but time had nearly run out for the men at Béxar.

If preparing the defense of Béxar was not difficult enough by itself, the political split between the governor and the General Council distracted the garrison from the task at hand. On January 27, Neill informed the council that he was aware of its actions and warned of their effect on Texas. "I have received your dispatches pr express and are truly astonished to fine your body in such a disorganized situation—Such Interuptions in the General Council of Texas have bad tendancies—they create distrust & alarm and at this critical period of our History are much to be lamented—I do hope however to hear of a reconciliation of matters,—Our govt. appears to be without a legitimate head, and unity of action is certainly necessary to answer the ends and to effect the objects contemplated by the consultation."

As a soldier of a republic, Neill enclosed "a copy of the proceedings of a meeting held" at Béxar on January 24, which he presided over, where the garrison expressed its support for Smith.[32] The men of the Alamo had chosen sides in the destructive squabbles of their government. The memorial, dated January 26, emphatically stated "we will support his Excellency Governor Smith in his unyielding and patriotic efforts to fulfill the duties, and to preserve the dignity of his office, while promoting the best interests of their country and people against all usurpations and the designs of selfish and interested individuals." The Béxar garrison spoke plainly to the issue of ignoring edicts by governing bodies whose authority they did not recognize. "That all attempts of the president and members of the Executive council, to annul the acts of, or to embarrass the officer appointed by the general convention, are deemed by this meeting, as anarchical assumptions of power to which we will not submit."

Furthermore, the memorial thanked Smith for his work, invited the rest of the army and country to disavow the council's action, and declared the Matamoros Expedition illegal. To make sure their view was known to all, the memorial was ordered published in the *Brazoria Gazette, Nacogdoches Telegraph,* and *Telegraph and Texas Register.*[33]

Members of the garrison had been expressing their personal support to Smith for several weeks. One of Smith's most outspoken supporters was Amos Pollard, the post surgeon at Béxar. Pollard offered encouragement to Smith, contending that the "tory party," meaning the council and its supporters, would not prevail. Speaking of the garrison's published memorial, the doctor told him, "you will see by our resolutions here that we are determined to support you at all hazards."[34]

In addition to choosing sides in the Smith-General Council feud, the Béxar garrison had made another important political decision. The November 7, 1835, Declaration of Causes had not settled the issue of independence from Mexico, but many engaged in the current struggle saw it only a matter of time before a permanent break was effected. Houston, an ally to Smith, expressed his view on the subject to an acquaintance within weeks of the Consultation, saying "You will learn that the Independence of Texas is the ultimate mark for which we strive, and the prize for which we battle!!!"[35] The governor also supported independence, favoring a split with Mexico and all Mexicans. The Goliad garrison helped bring the debate to a head when on December 20, 1835, it issued its own Declaration of Independence, predating the official document that would be issued more than two months later at Washington-on-the-Brazos. In a public memorial, the garrison resolved that "the former province and department of Texas is, and of right ought to be, a free, sovereign, and independent State" and "That as such, it has, and of right ought to have, all powers, faculties, attributes, and immunities of other independent nations."[36]

Independence gained favor in Béxar as well. Dr. Pollard told Smith that he intended to make sure that the four delegates elected to represent the town should understand "that if they vote against independence, they will have to be very careful on returning here."[37] Jameson described the garrison's two delegates as "both staunch Independence men & damn other than such."[38] Disagreement over independence further divided Texans because the supporters of the Matamoros Expedition, like Dr. James Grant whose land was located around Monclova and would lose it if Texas seceded, tended to maintain that they were acting as Mexican Federalists in support of the Constitution of 1824.

Much has been written about the fact that the Alamo was to fall with the garrison unaware that independence had been declared on Washington-on-the-Brazos. In truth, however, the men of the garrison had already declared their own independence from Mexico and fully expected their countrymen to do the same. Writing on March 3 toward the end of the Alamo siege, Travis reasserted the feelings of the Béxar garrison on independence in a letter to one of the members of the convention meeting at Washington-on-the-Brazos. "Let the Convention go on and made a declaration of independence, and we will then understand, and the world will understand, what we are fighting for," he wrote. "If independence is not declared, I shall lay down my arms, and so will the men under my command. But under the flag of independence, we are ready to peril our lives a hundred times a day, and to drive away the monster who is fighting us under a blood-red flag, threatening to murder all prisoners and make Texas a waste desert."[39] More than mere rhetoric, Travis's message reflects the fact that for many the goal of the revolt had changed from restoring the Constitution of 1824 to severing ties with Mexico and the establishing a separate republic.

The Béxar garrison gained its most famous member when David Crockett also arrived in early February. The former congressman from Tennessee, who had lost his seat in the fall election, had left the United States, reportedly telling his constituents that they could go to hell and he would go to Texas. He crossed into Mexico shortly after the first of the year and enlisted at Nacogdoches for six months as a volunteer in the Provisional Army of Texas along with a group of traveling companions. He had hoped to be elected as a delegate to represent that community but unfortunately missed the election. After spending several weeks hunting and exploring, Crockett rode into Béxar around February 8 and reported for duty. Tradition accords him the command of a group called his "Tennessee Mounted Volunteers" but in reality he chose, at least initially, to serve as a private in Captain William B. Harrison's company. Jameson notified Smith that the Tennessean had arrived, writing on February 11, "We now number one hundred and fifty strong Col Crockett & Col Travis both here & Col Bowie in command of the volunteer forces."

BÉXAR LOSES ITS COMMANDER

Although Crockett's arrival lifted the garrison's spirit, the temporary loss of their commander gave them reason for concern. Neill had fought to provide them with food, clothing, and pay, but his connection with the Alamo was about to come to an end. On February 11 Jameson reported to Smith that Neill had left for home, having received a message informing him of illness in his family. The garrison mourned the loss of their champion although he promised a hasty return. "There was a great regret at his departure by all of the men though he promised to be with us in 20 days at the furtherest."[40] Before leaving, Neill turned the post over to the next highest-ranking regular officer on the scene, Lt. Col. Travis, who had only been at the fort about a week and was a stranger to most of its defenders.

On February 12, the day after Béxar's post commander departed, Travis reported to Smith that "In consequence of the sickness of his family, Lt. Col. Neill left this Post, and has requested me to take Command of the Post." He reiterated that only about 150 men were in the town and lamented that the citizens of Texas had failed to respond to the present emergency. Part of the problem, he conceded, lay with the political unrest. He hoped "that all party dissention will subside, that our fellow Citizen will unite in the Common Cause and fly to the defence of the Frontier." In Travis's estimation, the post could be maintained with two hundred more men but he specified that they must be regulars for as he had previously told Houston, "militia and volunteers are but ill suited to garrison a town." In addition to more men, "Money, Clothing, and Provisions" were in great need. In reality, Travis was only repeating what Neill had been telling the governor for weeks.

Travis shared Bowie's sentiment about the necessity of holding Béxar. He exclaimed, "It is the key of Texas from the Interior without a footing here the enemy can do nothing against us in the colonies *now* that our coast is guarded by armed vessels." Although ill-prepared, the present garrison was "determined to sustain it as long as there is a man left; because we consider death preferable to disgrace, which would be the result of giving up a Post which was so dearly won, and thus opening the door for the Invaders to enter the Sacred Territory of the Colonies." Echoing Neill and Bowie's resolve to "die in these ditches [rather] than give it up to the enemy," Travis told the governor "I am determined to defend it to the last, and, should Bejar fall, your friend will be buried beneath its ruins."[41]

Even though vowing to die in its defense, Travis never sought command of the post. He had always wanted Smith to send Captain Forsyth's company to Béxar without him, thereby allowing him to continue raising the rest of his battalion of cavalry. Now Travis ironically found himself in command of a town and a fort. Worse for him still, many of the independent-minded volunteers failed to recognize his authority, something that threatened to split the garrison at a time when everyone acknowledged that the Centralists were mounting an attack on Texas.

The Béxar garrison, actually an amalgamation of independent companies, was not a cohesive force. Most were volunteers who had either stayed in town after Cos's defeat or new men who had arrived within the last month. Forysth's company, part of Travis's newly raised cavalry battalion, were regulars—but only in name as they lacked the training needed to turn them into professional soldiers. The volunteers at Béxar shared the common notion with nineteenth century citizen-soldiers that they had the right to elect their leaders, both civilian and military. Neill, the choice of the volunteers who stayed after the Battle of Béxar, had gained their respect and cooperation by assigning one of their own, Captain William Carey, to command the Alamo while he had maintained overall command of the town. Moreover, Neill had participated in the Battle of Béxar and Travis had not.[42]

Travis, who had experience with volunteers at both the Anahuac disturbances and the Siege of Béxar, knew he was in a "awkward & delicate" situation. As he explained to Smith in a February 13 letter describing his plight, "wishing to give satisfaction to the volunteers here & and not wishing to assume any command over them I issued an order for the election of an officer to command them with the exception of one company of volunteers that had previously engaged to serve under me." While correctly judging that his men would be jealous of their republican traditions, he did not anticipate the rancor his move would cause. "The volunteers being under a wrong impression, and ever ready to catch at any popular excitement, objected to Col Travis, and immediately named Col Bowie as their choice," wrote John Baugh, the post's adjutant. "An election was consequently ordered by Col. Travis and Bowie was Elected.—without opposition." Travis's reaction, wrote Baugh, was not positive. He would not "submit to the control of Bowie and he (Bowie) availing himself of his popularity among the volunteers seemed anxious to arrogate to himself the entire control." Instead of creating harmony, as Travis had hoped, the election split the garrison into factions.

Bowie proceeded to assert his newly acquired authority throughout the town. As Travis complained to the governor, "since his election he has been roaring drunk all the time; has assumed all command—& is proceeded in a most disorderly & irregular manner—interfering with private property, releasing prisoners sentenced by court martial & the civil court & turning everything topsy turvey." Baugh contended that Bowie had prevented citizens from leaving town and even threatened to use force against the Alcalde in order to obtain the release of prisoners from confinement. He reported that Travis, after having protested Bowie's actions, "has, as a last resort, drawn off his Troops to the Medina, where he believes he may be as useful as in the Garrison, at all events, save himself implication in this disgraceful business."

Travis appealed to Smith for assistance. Stung by the affair, he told the governor that only his honor and the need of his country kept him from taking his troops and immediately leaving Béxar. "I am unwilling to be responsible for the drunken irregularities of any man," he proclaimed. He repeated that he had not asked for the post and even pointed out that Smith had sent him there against his wishes. The townspeople liked him and he had their confidence. If the governor so ordered him to remain, he would, but only until an artillery officer could be sent to replace him. The situation had become unbearable and Travis desperately wanted to leave.[43]

The governor did not have time to act before he received a letter dated February 14, jointly written by Travis and Bowie, informing him that the issue of command had been resolved and order restored. "By an understanding of to day Col. J. Bowie has the command of the volunteers of the garrison, and Col. W. B. Travis of the regulars and volunteer cavalry. All general orders and correspondence will henceforth be signed [by] both until Col. Neill's return." The letter asked for money and reinforcements and repeated the warning that "the enemy will shortly advance upon this place." The warning proved true as Santa Anna and the Centralist forces would return to Béxar just nine days later.[44]

Chapter Six
The Battle

*Béxar was held by the enemy and it was necessary to open the door
to our future operations by taking it.*[1]
Antonio López de Santa Anna
1837 Manifesto

Something was happening! The pickets desperately tried to sound the alarm but their voices were lost in the shouts of the approaching columns. Soon they were swept away like driftwood on a beach by the rising tide. The garrison inside the Alamo woke abruptly from their sleep. Grabbing weapons and accouterments, men rushed from their quarters to defend the wall of the old mission. Some were defiant. Some were scared. All realized the gravity of their situation. Awakened, too, was the garrison's commander, Travis. With his slave Joe at his side, he rushed to the north wall, screaming "Give 'em hell boys! The Mexicans are upon us!"

The *soldados* were grateful that the garrison had been surprised. Perhaps they could reach the walls before the rebels did. Suddenly, though, fire erupted from the fortified compound, lighting up the darkness and sending pieces of jagged iron and lead through their ranks. Their officers drove the lines forward, knowing that what happened in the next few moments might very well determine the battle's outcome. Some *soldados* could not resist the urge to fire back against the rebels lining the top of the walls. One shot struck home on the north wall. The target was Travis, who fell to the ground with a bullet wound to his forehead. Lacking the promised reinforcements, the understrength garrison was now without a commander as well.

THE ALAMO UNDER SIEGE

The Centralist government renewed its campaign to suppress the revolt while the Texans feuded among themselves. Beginning in December, Santa Anna organized an expeditionary force that numbered approximately 6,500 men. Provisions and the pack animals to carry them were acquired through purchase and impressment. Recruits, some Yucatan Indians who did not speak Spanish, were pressed into service and hurriedly pressed forward. Santa Anna did not plan to wait until spring to return to Texas.

The Texans knew the basic outline of the Centralists' strategy: their spies had brought word of the impending advance in late January. Santa Anna intended to launch a two-pronged assault into Texas. One wing of the army, commanded by General José Urrea, was tasked with squelching Federalist support in the state of Tamaulipas before entering Texas. The Centralists feared that towns along the Rio Grande might revolt in support of the Federalists and cooperate with the rebels who were reportedly on their way to seize Matamoros. Once the region was secure, Urrea was to march northward on a path that would take him through Goliad and into the Anglo colonies. Santa Anna would accompany a larger wing of the army from the Rio Grande to Béxar. Once the town was back under Centralist control, these troops would march eastward. The rebels would then either be caught in a pincher movement or forced to flee to Louisiana in order to escape.

News of the Centralist advance had been relayed to the provisional government from Goliad as well as Béxar. Fannin had received news of the Centralist advance into Texas from the governor but discounted it because it came from Smith, explaining, "I suspect the Cause of the rumor."[2] But Fannin soon changed his mind and on February 16 wrote Robinson informing the lieutenant governor that the Centralist offensive was about to commence and for the government to "Send from twelve to fifteen hundred men to Béxar immediately." He explained his plans: "If General Houston does not return to duty on the expiration of his furlough [to treat with the Cherokees], and it meets your approbation, I shall make head quarters at Béxar, and take with me such force as can be spared."[3] Fannin's purpose for writing was to warn the government that the time for offensive operations against the towns on the Rio Grande had passed and that the frontier must now be defended.

The force assembled for the Matamoros Expedition was in disarray. Fannin remained at Presidio La Bahía near the town of Goliad. He had strengthened the old Spanish fort's defenses and renamed it Fort Defiance. The majority of the volunteers in the area remained with him but a number had chosen to follow Johnson and Grant, who had advanced southward to be closer to their objective. Their men had fanned out across the countryside to look for horses and supplies needed for the upcoming campaign. Urrea's task was thus made easier by the expedition's dispersal because he could find and defeat each in detail.

Johnson and thirty-four men had occupied the town of San Patricio, using its church and other buildings for quarters. Early on the morning of February 27, they were startled to find that Urrea and four hundred Centralist troops had entered the town. Urrea had left his main column and had force marched to San Patricio in order to catch Johnson by surprise. The plan succeeded and the Texans, scattered throughout the town, were unable to mount an effective defense. Urrea's soldiers killed eight of the insurgents and captured another thirteen, but Johnson and a few of his men escaped into the darkness. Fannin later learned of the attack from the survivors. Although this event occurred some distance from Béxar, it and subsequent activities conducted by Urrea had a serious effect on what happened at the former Spanish mission called the Alamo.

Santa Anna may have hoped to take the insurgents at Béxar by surprise. He had ordered his cavalry to push ahead, planning for them to enter the town before the rebels were aware of their presence, but the weather interfered. Upon reaching the Medina River, the Centralists discovered that recent rains had caused it to rise, making it impassable. Santa Anna arrived and his troops spent February 22 drying clothes and waiting for the river to go down.

His plan to seize the town with a swift raid spoiled, Santa Anna ordered the advanced elements of his army under General Ramirez y Sesma across the river on the morning of February 23. By mid-morning they reached Alazan Heights, a low line of hills just west of Béxar. Once there, Ramirez y Sesma ordered a halt for his troops to rest while the army joined him. He believed that the rebels had been alerted to his approach and were prepared to resist his entrance into the town. Several townspeople had spotted the Centralists, some of whom spread the alarm.

Word of the Centralists' approach stunned Béxar. Many residents had already headed into the countryside to escape the looming battle, the second the town had seen in less than three months. News of the actual arrival prompted even more Bexareños to make a speedy exodus from town. The members of the Béxar garrison reacted to the news by withdrawing across the San Antonio River to the Alamo. Families of the insurgents accompanied their relatives into the fortified compound for safety. A sentinel's report that the gleam of Mexican lance heads could be seen on the western horizon sped the exodus from town. Early that afternoon Santa Anna and his troops entered Béxar from the west and occupied its central plazas unopposed. A detachment was sent to check the other missions for the rebel forces, but they had abandoned the town and had taken refuge in the fortifications Jameson had worked so hard to prepare for them.

Travis and Bowie, apparently with less cooperation than that promised to Smith in their letter expressing their intention to share command, reacted to Santa Anna's sudden arrival by attempting to negotiate with the Centralist leader. Upon entering the civil plaza in town, Santa Anna had ordered a red flag raised over San Fernando Church to signify the Centralist administration's decision to conduct the campaign in Texas under the policy of "no quarter." Upon seeing the banner appear, Travis ordered a cannon fired at Béxar. Bowie sent Jameson out of the compound under a white flag with a message that expressed confusion over the meaning of the flag and cannon shot, asking if the Centralists had requested a truce. Jameson was told there would be no negotiating with the rebels but that they could surrender and throw themselves on the mercy of the government. Travis, learning that Bowie had sent Jameson without consulting him, sent Albert Martin out under another white flag to ask for terms under which the situation could be resolved. Martin, like Jameson before him, returned with the message that they must surrender immediately if they expected to be spared. With the enemy finally before them, Travis and Bowie managed to send a joint letter to Gonzales asking that reinforcements be sent to their aid at once.

The Béxar garrison's refusal to surrender initiated a traditional siege of the compound designed to soften up the fortification's defenses for an eventual assault. Only a portion of the Centralist force had accompanied Santa Anna to Béxar, the remainder were either with Urrea or still on the march. The Mexican general had approximately 1,600 with him when he arrived on February 23. His artillery train was relatively small, consisting of only eight guns: 2 eight pounders, 2 six pounders, 2 four pounders, and 2 seven-inch howitzers. Beginning on the afternoon of his arrival, his troops began constructing fieldworks across the river from the Alamo in which these pieces could be placed and his gunners protected from the enemy's fire. Over the next two weeks his troops constructed additional works to the south, east, and finally, north. As in any siege, his plan was to encircle the enemy's position in order to prevent the defenders' escape as well as to intercept reinforcements should they arrive to assist the besieged.

The garrison watched from the Alamo's walls as the siege progressed. As Jameson had indicated to both Houston and Smith, "Fortress Alamo" had not been constructed as a fort. In essence it was a fortified village whose structures were laid out around the perimeter of a three-acre rectangle. The individual huts and buildings had been connected in most places by walls, erected by the Spanish to deter Comanche raiders from entering the compound at will. Construction at the mission had begun in 1724 and continued until its closure in 1793. The central plaza of the mission compound

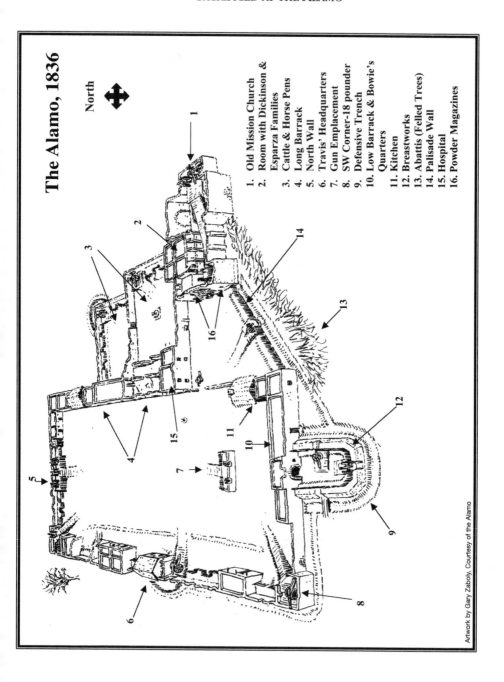

The Alamo, 1836

North

1. Old Mission Church
2. Room with Dickinson & Esparza Families
3. Cattle & Horse Pens
4. Long Barrack
5. North Wall
6. Travis' Headquarters
7. Gun Emplacement
8. SW Corner-18 pounder
9. Defensive Trench
10. Low Barrack & Bowie's Quarters
11. Kitchen
12. Breastworks
13. Abattis (Felled Trees)
14. Palisade Wall
15. Hospital
16. Powder Magazines

Artwork by Gary Zaboly, Courtesy of the Alamo

lay on a north-south axis, with the missionaries occupying the *convento* located on its eastern side and the neophytes or Indian converts occupying the individual huts located on its west side. A church was begun on the southeastern corner of the compound in 1744 but collapsed before it was completed. Around 1756, construction began on its replacement but it was never finished. Although the walls of the church had been raised by 1793, the building still lacked a roof.

The military occupation—first by the Spaniards and then by the Mexicans—marked a real effort to make the site more defensible. Numerous American incursions into Texas after 1800 had prompted Spanish officials to strengthen the gatehouse (called the Low Barrack) along the south wall of the compound as well as to build a watchtower several hundred yards to the east on a ridge overlooking Béxar. When the Texas Revolution erupted, Mexican military engineers under Cos had constructed earthen platforms around the compound on which they mounted artillery. A platform had even been constructed at the east end of the roofless church to guard the approach to the Alamo from that direction. The old *convento* had quartered troops for many years and had become known as the Long Barrack. The other structures around the perimeter housed officers and served as storerooms. A palisade, made of two rows of logs packed with earth in between them, ran from the corner of the Low Barrack to the corner of the church, closing off the one open space that had existed along the perimeter. A U-shaped palisaded redoubt had been constructed to protect the archway leading through the Low Barrack into the compound. Felled trees had been placed in front of the palisade, arranged so their sharpened branches pointed toward the attackers. Called an *abattis* in military terms, it served as a natural type of barbed wire. Although the walls of the church were four feet thick in some places and more than twenty feet high, the walls of the rest of the compound were only about a foot thick and less than half the height of the church.

The insurgents had inherited this fortified compound as a result of their victory over Cos in December. Jameson clearly saw its limitations as a fort and tried to make what changes he could with no money and few men willing to assist with rebuilding the fortifications. He left the gun emplacements that were already there. Approximately twenty-one pieces of artillery of various calibers were at his disposal, most of which he had tried to mount on the walls. The problem for the defenders was that the guns were mounted *en bar-bette*, meaning that they were high on the wall with their barrels extending over its top. The mounting worked well for any enemy located at some distance. However, it was possible for an attacking force to advance to a point where the barrels could no longer be depressed and brought to bear on them, making the guns useless. Without proper firing steps for the infantry who were to man the walls, the men had to expose themselves to the enemy's fire in order to fire themselves. Should the attackers make it under the guns and to the base of the walls, an *escalade* or assault by scaling was almost certain.

Both sides exhibited initiative during the first days of the siege. Small arms fire (musket and rifle) from inside the Alamo inflicted a number of casualties on the Centralist troops as they worked to erect their breastworks. Santa Anna sent a small force to seize a cluster of *jacales* located near the southwest corner of the compound that could be used as a forward post. The garrison skirmished with these troops throughout the afternoon before sallying out to burn the huts that night to prevent them from being used as shelter by the enemy. A few days later, another skirmish broke out just east of the Alamo when a fatigue party was sent out to collect wood and to clear a blocked *acequia* or irrigation ditch.

As the siege wore on, both sides relied on their artillery to harass their opponents. Exploding shells from the Centralists' two how-itzers made it dangerous for the garrison to venture out into the open. Solid shot from their field guns punched holes into the fort's stone walls and tore away wooden supports. Some of Santa Anna's officers believed that a breach could easily be made with heavier guns, forcing the defenders to concede defeat without having to assault the fort. For their part, the Alamo's cannoneers returned the fire when they could, even once striking the house Santa Anna was using as his quarters. The general, however, was away at the time.

The question of command of the Béxar garrison had finally been resolved. On February 24, Bowie had become so ill that he had to be confined to his quarters for the remainder of the siege. Travis took charge of the heretofore divided garrison. He issued his most famous appeal for help that day, addressed to "To the People of Texas & all Americans in the world—Fellow Citizens & Compatriots," in which he said:

> I am besieged by a thousand or more of the Mexicans under Santa Anna. I have sustained a continual Bombardment & cannonade for 24 hours & have not lost a man. The enemy has demanded a surrender at discretion, otherwise the garrison are to be put to the sword, if the fort is taken. I have answered the demand with a cannon shot, & our flag still waves proudly from the walls. *I shall never surrender or retreat.* Then, I call on you in the name of Liberty, of patriotism & every thing dear to the American character, to come to our aid with all dispatch. The enemy is receiving reinforcements daily & will no doubt increase to three or four thousand in four or five days. If this call is neglected, I am determined to sustain myself as long as possible & die like a soldier who never forgets what is due his own honor & that of his country. VICTORY or DEATH.[4]

The letter made its way eastward, finally reaching the Convention at Washington-on-the-Brazos, whose members ordered its public printing. Thus, Travis's stirring appeal gained an audience both inside and outside Texas.

Other appeals by Travis followed. Messengers apparently were able to pass through the incomplete siege lines without much difficulty. Alarmed by the Centralist presence at Béxar, officials directed reinforcements be forwarded as quickly as possible. The primary responsibility for aiding Travis fell to Major Robert M. Williamson, the commander of the Ranger Battalion authorized by the Consultation. On March 1, Williamson, who knew Travis, wrote his friend an encouraging message:

You cannot conceive my anxiety; today it has been four whole days that we have not the slightest news relative to your situation and we are therefore given over to a thousand conjectures regarding you. Sixty men have left this municipality, who in all probability are with you by this date. Colonel Fannin with 300 men and four pieces of artillery has been on the march toward Béxar three days now.

Tonight we await some 300 reinforcements from Wahington, Bastrop, Brazoria, and S. Felipe and no time will be lost in providing you assistance. . . .

P. S. For God's sake hold out until we can assist you— I remit to you with Major Bonham communication from the interim government. Best wishes to all your people and tell them to hold on firmly by their "wills" until I go there. —Williamson.—Write us very soon.[5]

By March 4, however, the siege lines had been closed because no message from Travis dated after March 3 was ever received.

Williamson's letter had been only partly correct regarding the number of reinforcements on their way to Béxar. His greatest error was that Fannin was not on his way as he thought. Fannin had received Travis's appeal and had even set off for Béxar, but had turned back. He reported to the lieutenant governor, "[On February 25,] we took up our line of March (about three hundred strong, and four pieces of artillery), towards Béxar, to the relief of those brave men now shut up in the Alamo." His men camped on the far side of the river after a somewhat difficult crossing and spent the night still in sight of Fort Defiance. His officers came to him in the morning and requested a meeting. He explained,

The Council of War consisted of all the commissioned officers of the command and it was unanimously determined, that, inasmuch as a proper supply of provisions and means of transportation could not be had; as it was impossible, with our present means, to carry the artillery with us, and as by leaving Fort Defiance without a proper garrison, it might fall into the hands of the enemy with the provisions, etc., now at Matagorda, Dimmitt's Landing and Cox's Point and on the way to meet us; and as by report of our spies (sent out by Col. Bowers) we may expect an attack upon this place, it was deemed expedient to return to this post and complete the fortifications . . . .[6]

Fannin wrote Robinson again on February 28 describing his own situation that he believed precarious. He expressed the hope that Texas was rushing to Travis's assistance, asking the question, "What must be the feelings of the Volunteers now shut up in Béxar?"[7]

Of the promised reinforcements, only Captain Albert Martin's Gonzalez Ranging Company is known with certainty to have made it to the Alamo in time. Martin, who had acted as Travis's messenger the day the siege began, had left Béxar and traveled to Gonzales. Once there he organized his neighbors into a relief column for the Béxar garrison. Thirty-two men strong, this company entered the Alamo early on the morning of March 1. Their arrival raised the number of the garrison to around two hundred or more.[8]

Santa Anna was aware that reinforcements were on their way to Travis. He, too, had been told that Fannin was marching from Goliad to lift the siege. On February 28, he ordered his cavalry, supported by a detachment of infantry, to march down the road to Goliad and intercept the rebels. No rebels were found because Fannin had turned back. Unable to locate Fannin or any other relief force, the column returned to Béxar.

Santa Anna received reinforcements of his own. He had sent word back to General Antonio Gaona to send ahead by rapid march an additional thousand troops, including the battalion of *Zapadores*. The column reached Béxar on the morning of March 3, causing much rejoicing among the troops already there. News of Urrea's victory at San Patricio raised the morale of Santa Anna's troops even higher. Travis, who was unaware that Santa Anna was already at Béxar, mistakenly believed the celebration marked the arrival of the Centralist general.

Santa Anna, who now had nearly 2,600 troops at his disposal, decided that the time had come to end the siege by force. He called his senior officers together to announce his decision and ask their opinion. Several agreed with him but others contended that the attack should not be carried out until two twelve-pounders, which were expected perhaps as early as March 7, arrived and opened a breach in the Alamo's wall. He may well have had two of Napoleon's maxims on his mind as he listened to his officers offer their opinions: (1) councils of war traditionally recommend the most timid course of action and (2) a general's duty is to bring glory to his nation even if it takes the blood of his men.[9] When the matter of prisoners came up, Santa Anna reminded them that it was their government's policy to offer no quarter to foreign invaders. He dismissed the gathering and had plans for the attack drawn up.

The Assault

It was customary for officers to be given written orders detailing how an attack was to be carried out. Colonel Juan Valentine Amador wrote down Santa Anna's instructions and distributed the copies to those charged with conducting the assault.[10]

> Army of Operations.
> General Orders of the 5th of March, 1836
> 2 o'clock P.M.—Secret
> To the Generals, Chiefs of Sections, and Commanding Officers:
>
> The time has come to strike a decisive blow upon the enemy occupying the Fortress Alamo. Consequently, His Excellency, the General-in-chief, has decided that, tomorrow, at 4 o'clock A.M., the columns of attack shall be stationed at musket-shot distance from the first entrenchments, reach for the charge, which shall commence, at a signal to be given with the bugle, from the North Battery.

The first column will be commanded by General Don Martín Perfecto Cos, and, in his absence, by myself. The Permanent Battalion of Aldama (except the company of Grenadiers) and the three right centre companies of the Active Battalion of San Luis, will compose this first column.

The second column will be commanded by Colonel Don Francisco Duque, and, in his absence, by General Don Manuel Fernandez Castrillón; it will be composed of the Active Battalion of Toluca (except the company of Grenadiers) and the three remaining companies of the Active Battalion of San Luis.

The third column will be commanded by Colonel José Maria Romero, and in his absence, by Colonel Mariano Salas; it will be composed of the Permanent Battalions of Matamoros and Jimenes.

The fourth column will be commanded by Colonel Juan Morales, and, in his absence, by Colonel José Minon; it will be composed of the light companies of the Battalions of Matamoros and Jimemes, and of the Active Battalion of San Luis.

His Excellency the General-in-chief will, in due time, designate the points of attack, and give his instructions to the Commanding Officers.

The reserve will be composed of the Battalion of Engineers and five companies of Grenadiers of the Permanent Battalion of Matamoros, Jimenens and Aldama, and the Active Battalion of Toluca and San Luis.

This reserve will be commanded by the General-in-chief, in person, during the attack; but Colonel Agustin Arnat [Amat] will assemble this party, which will report to him, this evening, at 5 o'clock, to be marched to the designated station.

The first column will carry ten ladders, two crow-bars, and two axes; the second, ten ladders; the third, six ladders; and the fourth, two ladders.

123

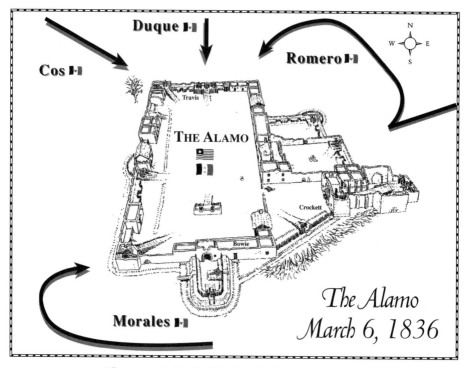

Duque

Cos

Romero

THE ALAMO

Travis

Crockett

Bowie

Morales

The Alamo
March 6, 1836

The men [with ladders] will sling their guns on their shoulders, to be enabled to place the ladders where ever they may be required.

The companies of Grenadiers will be supplied with six packages of cartridges to every man, and the centre companies with two packages and two spare flints. The men will wear neither overcoats or blankets, or anything that may impede the rapidity of their motions. The Commanding Officers will see that the men have the chin-straps of their caps down, and that they wear either shoes or sandals.

The troops composing the columns of attack will turn in to sleep at dark, to be in readiness to move at 12 o'clock at night.

Recruits deficient in instruction will remain in their quarters. The arms, principally the bayonets, should be in perfect order.

As soon as the moon rises, the centre companies of the Active Battalion of San Luis will abandon the points they are now occupying in the line, in order to have time to prepare.

The Cavalry, under Colonel Joaquin Ramírez y Sesma, will be stationed at the Alameda, saddling up at 3 o'clock A.M. It shall be its duty to scout the country, to prevent the possibility of escape.

The honor of the nation being interested in this engagement against bold and lawless foreigners who are opposing us, His Excellency expects that every man will do his duty, and exert himself to give a day of glory to the country, and of the gratification of the Supreme Government, who will know how to reward the distinguished deeds of the brave soldiers of the Army of Operations.[11]

The order was passed to Santa Anna's officers who prepared their men for the attack to come.

The Centralist troops were awakened around midnight and told to fall in. Their officers marched them silently to their positions and ordered them to lie on the ground and make no noise. A cold front had passed through the area several days earlier but had moved out. Even so, the men grew chilled on the cold, damp ground. Some dozed fitfully while they waited for the signal for the attack; others watched the fort for signs of movement that might indicate that the garrison had noticed their approach.

The Béxar garrison remained quiet, though. Santa Anna had ordered his cannon to cease fire and the silence had evidently lulled many to sleep. Sentinels had been placed outside the walls to sound the alarm in case of a surprise attack but either they failed to see the enemy move into position or they, too, slept. Travis had retired to his quarters located along the west wall. As far as he and his men knew, tomorrow would bring yet another day under siege.

The attack began prematurely. As the eastern horizon began to lighten, an anxious Centralist soldier cried out. Soon shouts of "Viva Santa Anna" and "Viva La Republica" were taken up along the line. Santa Anna, who was with the reserves at his northern most earthwork reacted to the shouts by immediately giving orders to commence the assault before the garrison had time to react.

Morales's column headed toward the palisade to draw the attention of the defenders positioned along the Alamo's south wall. Its task was to keep that section of the fort occupied while the main attacks took place elsewhere. Having made its demonstration, the column moved off to the southwest to take shelter behind a stone building that the garrison had not been able to destroy when they burned the *jacales*. There they reorganized and then rushed the southwest bastion of the fort.

Romero's column advanced from the east but soon encountered trouble. Fire from the artillery mounted on the back of the church ripped through its ranks. Additionally, a blocked *acequia* located on the eastern flank of the fort created a watery obstacle that impeded its progress. The column drifted to the north, away from the devastating fire of the church and the flooded ground.

Duque's column advanced from the north. The cannon fire from the Alamo also opened gaps in his line. Castrillón stepped forward to take command when Duque was wounded in the thigh. The men of his column pressed forward, though, and reached the north wall.

Cos's column came from the northwest. His objective may have been the west wall but he apparently struck Duque's right flank and the two columns merged for a time.

Startled awake by the sound of the attack, the garrison rushed from its quarters to take up positions along the walls. The attackers seemed to be coming from all directions. Travis, accompanied by his slave named Joe, raced to the north wall. He fired over the wall but reeled back mortally wounded when a musket ball struck him in the forehead. The Béxar garrison was without a commander.

The men of the garrison would fight on for some time, but the battle had been decided at this point. Scattered along the Alamo's wall and inside its building, the defenders battled against their attackers in a number of small, desperate, independent actions. The darkness and the thick smoke from burnt powder prevented a clear view of what was happening around them. Although some stepped forward to lead these pockets of resistance, no one organized a unified defense. It was an impossible task, however, given that the Centralist troops had already reached the fort's walls and were beginning to scale them. The Alamo's guns could not be depressed to fire at the troops massed at the base of the walls. Travis's death had already proven that firing from atop the walls exposed the garrison to the enemy's deadly fire. Anyone armed with a hunting rifle found himself at a disadvantage due to the limited visibility and time needed to load and fire. Once the Centralists began to top the wall and pour into the compound, the defenders had little choice but to seek shelter inside the buildings from where they could continue the fight.

Watching from his position to the north, Santa Anna believed that the reserves were needed and ordered them into the battle. They struck the north wall and entered the fort with Castrillón. Romero's men forced their way into the stock pens on the east side of the compound. Cos's men fanned out along the west wall and broke and pushed their way through blocked doors and windows. The Centralist soldiers on the wall and in the compound soon found themselves in grave danger from their own comrades. Fellow soldiers firing out of the darkness began to kill and wound those who had rushed ahead. Some Centralist officers later attributed the majority of their casualties to friendly fire rather than from the defenders.

Clearing the walls of the defenders had gained the Centralists an important advantage: they now had control of the fort's guns. Officers quickly ordered their men to turn the guns inward. Once repositioned and loaded, the pieces were used against their previous owners who had fallen back into the Long Barrack. Cannonballs punched holes in the stone walls and sent jagged fragments of rock flying throughout its rooms. In the end, though, the Centralist troops entered the building and cleared it with their bayonets.

The *soldados* fought their way into other buildings as well. They found Bowie in his sickbed in a Low Barrack room and killed him where he lay. They then turned the guns against the church. Once the doorway had been cleared, Centralist troops rushed in and killed the men working the guns on the elevated platform. Part of this action was witnessed by women and children whose quarters were in the church.

The fighting spread beyond the walls. A number of defenders were pushed out of the fort and tried to make their way to the road to Gonzales. Unknown to them, Santa Anna had prepared for such a contingency. According to the after-action report of Ramírez y Sesma, more than fifty members of the garrison died just southeast of the fort, killed by the lancers who lay in wait for them.

Centralist soldiers inside the Alamo warily searched through the rooms looking for survivors. Officers found Joe, who had returned to Travis's quarters after his master's death. They also located a number of women and children hidden throughout the various rooms of the fort. These people, considered non-combatants, were taken into town and later interviewed by Santa Anna that afternoon before being released.

Others were not so fortunate. The search of the fort turned up a handful of the garrison members who had managed to survive the carnage. Although asked by Castrillón to spare them, Santa Anna cited the Tornel Decree and ordered these men executed. A story circulated that two of the garrison's best known members, Crockett and Bonham, were among this handful of prisoners who were denied quarter.[12]

REMEMBER THE ALAMO!

The Centralists' campaign continued. To the east, Urrea and four hundred Centralist troops found Grant and twenty-six of his supporters at Agua Dulce Creek on March 2 and killed fourteen and took another six prisoner, whom Urrea ordered executed. Survivors carried word of the disaster to Goliad where the news caused near panic to break out. With Johnson defeated, Grant dead, and Urrea on his way to Goliad, the contentious Matamoros Expedition was about to come to a tragic close.

Fannin at Fort Defiance had learned that colonists in the path of Urrea's advance had requested help. On March 10, he sent Amon B. King and a small force with wagons to collect the families and escort them back to Goliad. King found that the Centralist force in the area was greater than first believed and asked Fannin to send help while he took refuge in the old mission at Refugio. Fannin dispatched William Ward, commander of the Georgia Battalion, to assist King. Ward's arrival at Refugio sparked a disagreement over command between the two officers. The squabbling caused the insurgents to break into several smaller detachments, each of which was subsequently defeated and its survivors captured by Urrea's troops. At Golaid, Fannin waited in vain for the return of these missing detachments.

The Texans finally had met at Washington-on-the-Brazos and formed a new provisional government. The delegates declared independence on March 2, abandoning any attempt to cooperate with Mexican Federalists in reestablishing the Federal Constitution of 1824 as the law of the land. Members set about creating the apparatus of a new republican government. One of the first orders of business was to produce a constitution for the new republic. Smith, who hoped that the Convention would investigate the actions of the General Council, found the delegates had no desire to look into his feud with the council that had been so destructive.

The Convention took up the matter for Texas's defense and reappointed Houston as the army's commander. This time, however, his authority extended over all troops, including those currently in the field. Houston left Washington-on-the-Brazos on March 6 to take charge of the effort to lift the siege at Béxar. He arrived at Gonzales on March 11 and found more than three hundred volunteers, among them J.C. Neill, ready to march to Travis's aid. That same day, though, two rancheros from Béxar arrived with word of the Alamo's destruction. Houston initially had the two men held as spies but the arrival of Susanna Dickinson and Joe confirmed the sad news.

Houston decided to abandon Gonzales and withdraw to the east. He sent orders to Goliad ordering Fannin to evacuate the fort and withdraw to Victoria where he would find Houston. On March 13, Houston burned Gonzales and marched eastward, a move that spread terror through Texas as families abandoned their homes and fled to escape the Centralist advance. On March 17, Houston crossed the Colorado River, the same day officials hurriedly abandoned Washington-on-the-Brazos. On March 20, Houston camped near the town of Columbia. On March 28, he passed through San Felipe. Two days later he arrived at Groce's Plantation on the Brazos River, where he encamped his army for nearly two weeks as he gathered men and supplies.

Dissatisfaction ran through his camp because many disapproved of his Fabian strategy of falling back and avoiding a battle with the enemy. As proponents of the frontier defense had warned, the loss of Béxar had brought the war into the heart of the Anglo settlements.

The war news was to get worse. Fannin had received Houston's orders to abandon Goliad but was reluctant to leave before the detachments he had sent to help to evacuate the colonists at Refugio rejoined him. Time, however, had run out. On March 18, he prepared his command to leave Fort Defiance when word arrived that Urrea's vanguard was approaching. Instead of departing immediately, he allowed his men to engage in a day of inconclusive skirmishing. He finally left the fort the next morning, carrying what supplies he could in ox carts. After traveling only a few miles, Fannin ordered a halt on the prairie in sight of Coleto Creek, disregarding his officers' warning that they should continue on to the safety of its bank. The decision proved to be unwise because elements of Urrea's cavalry dashed ahead and seized the tree line. His situation was exactly opposite of what it had been at the Battle of Concepcíon back in November: here the enemy was protected by cover and he and his men were caught in the open. Instead of attempting to drive the enemy from the creek before they were reinforced, Fannin ordered his men to form a square and dig breastworks. The Centralist cavalry was joined by Urrea with infantry. Casualties mounted inside the earthworks. That night the command voted against forcing their way through the Centralists' line because it would mean abandoning the wounded, which included their commander. Any chance of a break out was lost on the next morning when Urrea received reinforcements who had brought several pieces of artillery with them. Another meeting was held in which Fannin was authorized to surrender the command if the Centralists would treat them as prisoners of war. Urrea explained he had no authority to offer such terms but agreed to press their request for clemency. Satisfied that he and his men would be treated fairly, Fannin capitulated. Marched back to Fort Defiance and kept there for a week, more than four hundred members of Fannin's command were taken out and shot on Palm Sunday, March 27. The wounded, including Fannin, were executed inside the fort.

The campaign to subdue Texas seemed to be going exceedingly well from Santa Anna's point of view. Béxar had been retaken, the Matamoros Expedition had been crushed, and the rebels were on the verge of being either pushed into Louisiana or annihilated in battle. Emboldened by what appeared to be easy victories, he grew overconfident and careless. Learning that members of the *ad interim* government were at Harrisburg, he set off with a mounted force of five hundred men to capture the rebel's leaders. He crossed the Brazos River near Fort Bend on April 11 in pursuit of the *ad interim* government. He reached Harrisburg on April 15 but found they had already left. Santa Anna claimed the town was burning when he arrived but the Texans were ready to believe that his men had set the fire.

Houston had learned that Santa Anna had passed through Harrisburg. While he had been reluctant to engage an entire wing of the Centralist army in battle, the chance to catch Santa Anna ahead of his main force with only a small detachment seem too good of an opportunity to let pass. On April 17, Houston marched through Harrisburg. The next day he camped at White Oak Bayou and learned Santa Anna was near. On April 19, Santa Anna arrived at Morgan's Point and Houston crossed Buffalo Bayou: both were approaching a bend of the San Jacinto River.

The two forces found themselves only about a mile apart on the afternoon of April 20. Houston's men clamored for immediate action and he allowed them to skirmish with the enemy with the warning they were not to bring on a full-scale battle. Santa Anna, who realized he was outnumbered, sent word to his main army to forward reinforcements as quickly as possible. Commanded by Cos, the 650 reinforcements arrived at Santa Anna's camp on the morning of April 21. Santa Anna, himself having spent an anxious night waiting for reinforcements to arrive, allowed his troops to rest.

Houston, who had earlier written Fannin, "it is better to do well, *late*; than *never!*," was about to prove the truth of the maxim. He slept past noon. He found his army ready to fight when he awoke. The two forces were as relatively equal as he could expect: he commanded around 1,000 troops while the Centralists numbered about 1,300.

Houston must have been struck by the obvious similarity of his present location to the battleground where he had fought under General Jackson at Horseshoe Bend twenty-three years earlier. The Creeks had occupied the inside of an old river meander just like Santa Anna's troops did here in a bend of the San Jacinto River. Jackson had trapped his enemy by sending John Coffee and his men to line the riverbank opposite the enemy's encampment to block the Indians' escape. Houston had sent Deaf Smith to destroy the bridge over Buffalo Bayou, an action that cut off the Centralists' route of retreat. Jackson had made the terrain work to his advantage and so did the man who had looked to Old Hickory as a mentor.

Once Houston gave the order the Texans formed for battle and marched across the open plain separating them from Santa Anna's camp. The Centralist pickets had been withdrawn to feed their horses and eat something themselves shortly before the Texans commenced their attack. Although some of the *soldados* gave the alarm as the Texans approached, Houston's men rolled over the pile of packs and other equipment that formed an improvised breastwork. The organized battle lasted less than twenty minutes but the killing continued for hours. A number of Santa Anna's men fled toward Vince's Bridge but found it destroyed and escape impossible. Shouting "Remember the Alamo" and "Remember La Bahía," the Texans pursued the fleeing Centralists and killed them in their tracks. The casualty list tells the story: the Centralists lost 630 killed with 730 falling prisoner to the Texans while the Texans had lost 9 killed and had 30 wounded. The deaths of the Béxar garrison and others lost at the Alamo, Goliad, Auga Dulce, and Refugio had been avenged.

On April 22, the Battle of San Jacinto took on an even greater significance for Houston when Santa Anna was brought in by scouts who had found him hiding along the banks of Buffalo Bayou. Many in camp called for his execution, but Houston recognized that Santa Anna's capture gave the new government a potentially important hostage. Houston and the captured Mexican leader agreed to an armistice. On May 14, the provisional government of the Republic of Texas and Santa Anna signed the Treaty of Velasco that recognized Texas's independence and ended hostilities between the two nations. Although the Mexican government refused to accept these claims, Texas had effectively seceded from Mexico.

Some journalists had tried to compare my campaigns to those of Napoleon and my enemies hoped that that of Texas would be as disastrous to me as of Russia was to the Corsican hero.[13]

Antonio López de Santa Anna

1837 Manifesto

Conclusion

❦❧

D id the Béxar garrison sacrifice itself on the altar of Texas Liberty? This belief is imbedded in the tale of the Alamo even though William P. Zuber's oft repeated tale of the line in the sand has fallen into question. The traditional story contends that Travis and his men willingly stayed within the walls of the Alamo, certain of death, in order to give General Houston time to build the army that would save Texas. In retrospect, the defense of the Alamo occupied Santa Anna's wing of the Centralist Army and allowed the Convention at Washington-on-the-Brazos to conduct the important business of nation building. Houston, however, did not begin to organize his forces until nearly a week after the funeral pyres at Béxar burned out. Thus, Houston made no use of the time gained by the Béxar garrison. "Remember the Alamo!," though, became his rallying cry.

Traditionalists need not be concerned that I am suggesting that the Béxar garrison did not make the ultimate sacrifice by remaining at the Alamo. Nevertheless, it appears that they died still expecting help to arrive instead of resigning themselves to the inevitable slaughter. The bickering between their countrymen, whose different motives prevented agreement on a single course of action, prevented a successful frontier defense and allowed the Centralists access to the American colonies. Left largely on its own, the Béxar garrison held out as long as it could before being overwhelmed on the morning of March 6, 1836. Although killed by soldiers of Mexico's Centralist government, the Béxar garrison was doomed by the political infighting that raged among Texas's revolutionary leaders.

Appendix A

BARRAGAN DECREE

Office of the First Secretary of State, Interior Department.

His Excellency the President *pro tem* of the Mexican United States to the inhabitants of the Republic. Know ye, that the General Congress has decreed the following:

Art. 1. The present government of the states shall continue, notwithstanding the time fixed by the constitution may have expired; but shall be dependent for their continuance in the exercise of their attributes upon the Supreme Government of the nation.

Art. 2. The legislatures shall immediately cease to exercise their legislative functions: but before dissolving (and those which may be in recess meeting for the purpose) they shall appoint a Department Council, composed, for the present, of five individuals, chosen either within or without their own body, to act as a council to the governor; and in case of vacancy in that office, they shall propose to the Supreme General Government three persons possessing the qualifications hitherto required; and until an appointment be made, the gubernatorial powers shall be exercised by the first on the list who is not an ecclesiastic.

Art. 3. In those states where the legislature cannot be assembled within eight days, the Ayuntamiento of the capital shall act in its place, only for the purpose of electing the five individuals of the Department Council.

Art. 4. All judges and tribunals of the states, and the administration of justice, shall continue as hitherto, until the organic law relative to this branch can be formed. The responsibilities of the functionaries which could only be investigated before Congress, shall be referred to and concluded before the Supreme Court of the nation.

Art. 5. All the subaltern officers of the state shall also continue for the present (the places which are vacant, or which may be vacated, not to be filled), but they, as well as the officers, revenues, and branches under their charge, remain subject to, and at its disposal

135

of, the Supreme Government of the nation, by means of their respective Governor.

>Palace of the Federal Government in Mexico, Oct. 3d, 1835
>Miguel Barragan, [Acting President]
>D. Manuel Diez de Bonilla[1]

Appendix B

❧❦

THE TORNEL DECREE

MEXICO

WAR AND NAVY DEPARTMENT

Circular. The government has received information that, in the United States of North America, meetings are being called for the avowed purpose of getting up and fitting out expeditions against the Republic of Mexico, in order to send assistance to the rebels, foster the civil war, and inflict upon our country all the calamities, by which it is followed. In the United States, our ancient ally, expeditions are now organized similar to that headed by the traitor Jose Antonio Mexia and some have even set out for Texas. They have been furnished with every kind of ammunition, by means of which the revolted colonies are enabled to resist and fight the nation from which they received but immense benefits. The government is also positively informed that these acts, condemned by the wisdom of the laws of the United States, are also reported by the general government, with which the best intelligence and greatest [tear in paper]ony still prevail. However, as these adventurers and speculators have succeeded in escaping the penalties inflicted by the laws of their own country, it becomes necessary to adopt measures for their punishment. His excellency the president ad interim, anxious to repress these aggressions which constitute not only an offense to the sovereignty of the Mexican nation, but also to evident violation of international laws as they are generally adopted, has ordered the following decrees to be enforced.

Foreigners landing on the coast of the republic or invading its territory by land, armed with the intention of attacking our country, will be deemed pirates and dealt with as such, being citizens of no nation presently at war with the republic, and fighting under no recognized flag.

All foreigners who will import either by sea of land, in the places occupied by the rebels, either arms or ammunition of any kind for the use of them, will be deemed pirates and punished as such.

I send to you these decrees, that you may cause them to be fully executed.

> TORNEL.[2]
> Mexico 30th Dec. 1835

Appendix C

❦

E. Hoyt, *Practical Instructions of Military Officers*
(Greenfield, MÀ: John Denio, 1811), 296-301.
CHAPTER XII
Of the attack of redoubts, field-forts, villages, and other
detached posts.

There are two methods of attacking fortified posts; one by regular siege, in which the approaches are made with caution and under the cover of works; the other by assaults, or *coup de main*, where the assailants, by sudden and furious effort, attack without any cover. The latter only will be treated in this chapter.

The attack of a post, by a *coup de main*, when well fortified, is at all time critical, but more especially so when it is garrisoned by well disciplined men, under the command of brave, skillful, and experienced officers. Nevertheless attacks of this kind generally succeed, and sometimes when there is no remissness in the garrison; but these successes are generally to be imputed to some relaxation of duty, which is very apt to prevail in strong posts, particularly in those at a considerable distance from the enemy.

Before the officer undertakes an enterprise of this kind, he should carefully reconnoitre the post and environs, or employ some person on whose skill and judgment he can place the utmost confidence; but the former is much the safest; for plans, views, and reports, however accurately drawn, can never give so perfect a knowledge of a place as an actual examination.

Having obtained the necessary information, he will form his plan of attack and lay it before the commanding general for his approbation.

When the project originates with the general, he does not always give positive orders to an officer to take the command, but suggests it to such as he judges best calculated for the enterprise, and accepts of the one who volunteers his service. The officer being fixed upon, he should, if time and circumstances will permit, reconnoitre the place to gain a more accurate knowledge of the situation and proposed plan of attack.

As the situation and strength of posts are infinitely various, no certain rules can be given for forming plans of attack. These are best acquired from the exploits of brave and skillful officers. A few examples of this kind will be cited in this chapter.

The choice of men for these enterprises is one of great importance for on them the success very much depends. In general, none but volunteers of determined bravery ought to be taken; men who are obedient, well disciplined, and have no colds upon them, which might cause them to cough and thereby give the enemy notice of their approach.

The men being selected, they must be carefully inspected, to see that their arms, equipments, &c. are in complete order, and that nothing is wanting to ensure success. If the post is fortified with an earthen parapet, a few spades and pick-axes will be necessary; if fraised [angled stakes] or palisaded [vertical stakes], light axes must be procured; and if covered with masonry, timber, or fascines, ladders must be furnished for scaling.

It is useful to make one or two false attacks to favor the true ones, the assailants therefore must be divided into as many divisions or platoons as there are attacks to be made, and each commanded by an officer, accompanied by a resolute sergeant and corporal. The guides that are employed to conduct the parties must be examined concerning every thing that is necessary to be known, and particularly about the roads on which troops are to advance. In the choice of guides, much caution is necessary; they should be brave, discerning, and intelligible. Animated with the hopes of gain, they may undertake without the requisite qualifications; others, perhaps hired by the enemy, engage with a design to lead the party into ambuscade, where they escape and leave it to be cut in pieces. There is great danger in trusting to deserters from the enemy, and they ought never to be confided in, excepting where the greatest caution is used; for having once been treacherous, they will probably continue so.

When an officer has selected such as appear qualified, he is to inform them that they will be instantly put to death if they are not true and faithful. He may as a further security, require their wives and children as hostages of their fidelity, and when the party marches, the guides may be separated and placed under the care of trusty non-commissioned officers, who are to never lose sight of them. If conducted by a deserter, it may be proper while it is dark, to have him fastened with a cord, and led by a non-commissioned officer.

The night being the most proper for *coups-de-main*, the party should march in the evening, as silently as possible, making the use of such of the precautions, pointed out in the chapter on *secret marches*, as the commander judges necessary to ambuscades. Where the roads are narrow it will be best to march by files, in close order, and the men must be charged not to speak, cough, or spit, on any accounts. Before the party arrives at the post, a *watchword* should be given to the officers and soldiers, that they may be able to distinguish friends from enemies in the dark.

When the party approaches near the post, it may be ordered to halt and lie close upon the ground, while the commander makes such further arrangements as are necessary for the attack. If a patrol of the enemy appears, the party must continue close upon the ground, profoundly silent, and permit it to pass. If the patrol approaches the place where the party is concealed, the commander should endeavor to seize it, without noise, but if the patrol discovers the party before it can be seized, the commander must instantly give the order or signal for the attack, on which the whole advance according to the prescribed plan, before the enemy can get under arms; or if he judges it imprudent to attack, he may retire without attempting to carry the post.

In fortified places, the most favorable points of attack are the salient angles, for these are not so easily defended as the other parts. If the post to be attacked is a square redoubt, with a dry ditch and parapet of earth, the front rank must carry their spades and pick-axes in one hand and their muskets in the other, and on arriving at the counterscrap, both ranks must instantly leap into the ditch, where they will be covered from the fire of the place; but the rear rank must take care that they do not leap upon the bayonets of the front rank. Having got into the ditch, the scarp and parapet must be sapped to facilitate the mounting, and if the parapet fraised, passages must be made sufficient for the men to pass, by breaking or cutting them away as quick as possible. The men will then mount the parapet, rush upon the garrison with fixed bayonets, and attack all who attempt resistance.

When the scraps and parapets are faced with stone or timber, they cannot easily be mounted without scaling ladders. If an officer is to attack a post thus fortified, he must provide ladders for part of his men, and they must be made so long as to reach the top of the parapet when set up with the proper slope. The stoutest soldiers will carry the ladders with the left arm passing through the second step, holding them upright to their sides, and the short below, that they may not dislocate their shoulders in leaping into the ditch. The front rank of each division, provided with ladders, and their arms in the right hand, will lead on, followed by the rear rank, leap into the ditch, and place the ladders against the parapet within a foot of each other, with a proper slope.

The ladders being placed, as many as can should mount, and rush upon the enemy with swords and bayonets. If a leading man happen to be overturned, the next should take care not to be forced down by his body, but help him to pass between the ladders, and immediately mount in his place.

The success of an attack by scaling is infallible if the garrison is unprepared, and all sides are scaled at once. If the enemy are ready the success will be more certain if the assailants shower grenades upon them, and have supporting parties a little back to divide their fire.

If the place to be attacked has a few feet of water in the ditch, it should not prevent the men from entering, in the manner mentioned; but if the ditch is full, the soldiers should carry fascines of small branches, well bound, and as large as is convenient for carriage, to fill up the ditch, or make a kind of bridge over which they can pass and scale the parapet.

Many other methods of filling the ditch are proposed by engineers, but that mentioned seems to be preferable, as the men can easily carry the fascines, and when placed in front, they are a good defence against musketry, and are easily and expeditiously placed in the ditch.

If the approaches to a post are defended by *chevaux-de-frise*, they must be cut down with axes, or removed out of the way. If the post is surrounded by abattis, passages must be cur through, or if they are dry they may be set on fire, by throwing among them fascines lighted at one end. When fired, the assailants may fall back out of the light, to avoid the musketry of the garrison. If *chauss-trapes* are scattered around the place, they may be swept away by dragging trees over the ground. But obstructions of this nature cannot be wholly removed when a place is to be surprised, as the noise will necessarily alarm the garrison.

When a detached building is attacked, the assailants must endeavor to set it on fire by lighting faggots, dipped in rosin, or with fire balls. These may be thrown in at the windows or doors, if they can be forced open. The men may be covered in their approaches, by a kind of *mantelet* of plank, fixed upon cart or waggon wheels. Under the cover of several of these mantelets, a beam may be carried to the houses, suspended by ropes to a kind of *gin*, in imitation of a battering ram. With this, a breach may soon be made in the house, and the garrison will be glade to capitulate.

By such means an officer will carry a fortified house with the loss of but few soldiers; and as their blood is precious, he will prefer these and similar modes of attack, and use every mean that will contribute to their preservations.

Appendix D

PRINCIPLES OF WAR

The following is a brief analysis of the Siege and Battle of the Alamo according to the principles of war as recognized by military historians.[3]

Objective. **Every campaign must have a clear achievable objective.**

Government: The Centralist strategy clearly called for a two-pronged advance into Texas aimed at the Anglo colonies. The campaign was intended either to defeat the insurgents or to drive them out of Texas. The Centralist column followed the two main roads leading through Texas, meaning that Béxar (to the west) and Goliad (to the east) had to be recaptured. The plan guaranteed that there would be engagements at these two locations unless the insurgents chose to evacuate.

Insurgents: The civil and military leaders of Texas were divided and could not decide on a single course of action. The very purpose of the revolt was debated as proponents of the Constitution of 1824 tried to stave off calls for independence. Although Béxar and other posts were captured, early success dissolved into chaos. Some in Texas demanded that frontier defense (Béxar and Goliad) be strengthened but others planned to take the war deeper into Mexico with an expedition to Matamoros. The lack of unity left the insurgents ill-prepared for the Centralist counterattack.

Offensive. **Only offensive action achieves decisive results.**

Government: The Centralist plan placed the insurgents on the defense, meaning that the government's army controlled the initiative. A well-conducted offense allows the attackers more options as to when, where, and how to advance.

Insurgents: The insurgents seized the initiative early in the conflict and achieved numerous military successes. Momentum was lost after the Battle of Béxar as political feuds divided the rebels. The Matamoros Expedition, which would have carried the war to the Centralists, bogged down and divided the Texas military into factions. With the initiative lost, the insurgents were forced to react to the Centralist advance.

***Simplicity.* Combat, by its nature, works against complex plans.**

Government: The overall Centralist strategy was clear and simple. Santa Anna's orders for the attack on the Alamo, which were clear and simple, followed established military guidelines.

Insurgents: The Texan leaders could not agree on a single objective. Two competing military goals emerged: (1) defend the frontier and (2) carry the war to the Centralists by advancing on Matamoros. The insurgents' limited resources did not allow them to support a dual purpose strategy. As for the defense of the Alamo, the fortifications themselves were complicated which worked against the garrison tasked with defending the compound.

***Unity of Command [Command of Control].* A commander must have control of his troops in order to direct their actions.**

Government: The Centralists inherited an organized military force with a well-organized command structure. At the Battle of the Alamo, Santa Anna's orders clearly state the chain of command , even indicating who will take over each attack column in case its leader is killed or wounded.

Insurgents: The civil government had split into two separate bodies, each of which refused to cooperate with the other. The military was divided over the issue of regular vs. volunteer command. The commanding general of the regular army was unavailable for the month of February. The volunteers in the field had broken into rival factions, loyal to the governor, general council, or, in some cases, loyal only to their local commander. In Béxar, the garrison had a history of independent thinking and action leading back to Austin's command of the army. The Travis-Bowie feud widened the rift that already existed between what amounted to independent companies consolidated into a single battalion. Bowie's illness removed a charismatic leader. The garrison appeared to have no clear chain of command on March 6. Travis's death essentially ended any hope for a unified defense on the morning of the battle.

Mass [Concentration]. **Numerical superiority applied at specific points is needed to break the enemy's line.**

Government: Santa Anna and Urrea were able to bring numerically superior forces against the enemy wherever they found them. Santa Anna was able to achieve at least a ten to one advantage over the Alamo garrison.

Insurgents: The insurgents, whose military was yet to be fully developed, were unable to achieve numerical superiority against the Centralists.

Economy of forces. **Unengaged forces must be kept small in order to achieve mass.**

Government: Less than one half of the army assembled by the Centralists were used in the campaign against Béxar and Goliad; the remainder were en route. Although a greater concentration of forces may have quickened the pace of the campaign, logistical considerations prevented the massing of more troops in an area than local resources could support at one time.

Insurgents: The lack of organization, difference of opinion over an objective, and no unified command and control made the allocation of troops difficult.

Maneuver. **Rapid and or unexpected movement brings strategic and/or tactical advantage.**

Government: Santa Anna and Urrea pushed their columns hard, thereby arriving at their objectives sooner than thought possible by the enemy.

Insurgents: Lacking unity of purpose and command, the insurgents assumed static positions.

Surprise. **Surprise causes the enemy to have to react to the unexpected, increasing the chance that he will make mistakes that can be exploited.**

Government: Both Urrea and Santa Anna were able to achieve surprise by making rapid advances. Both, too, achieved surprise in predawn assaults.

Insurgents: Divided as to course of action and entrenched in static positions, the insurgents had little or no opportunity to achieve surprise.

Security. **It is important to guard against being surprised by the enemy.**

Government: Both the Centralists and the insurgents had knowledge of their enemy because the conflict was a civil war in which the opponents knew each other and the terrain over which the campaign was to be conducted. At Béxar, Santa Anna was able to gain intelligence about the Alamo and its garrison through residents loyal to the government.

Insurgents: The disorganized condition of the insurgents hampered any systematic gathering of information about the Centralist intentions. Nevertheless, reports were received regularly from *Tejanos* who supported the revolt but the revolt's leaders were unable to respond in a meaningful manner. Johnson and Grant's removal of the Béxar garrison's horse herd prevented Neill from sending out routine patrols. Once the siege began, the besieged garrison had limited assess to news from the outside. Travis's belief that Santa Anna did not arrive in town until March 3 demonstrates the garrison's lack of up to date intelligence. The apparent failure of the Travis' pickets to detect the Centralist troops massing before the Alamo on the morning of March 6 was a fatal breach of security.

To this list can be added the following important principle:

Morale. **High morale can overcome adversity by increasing fighting spirit.**

Government: The Centralists began the campaign with a good chance to crush the revolt in Texas. Urrea's victory at San Patricio bolstered morale throughout Centralist forces.

Santa Anna believed that a victorious storming for the Alamo would instill his men with pride; however, the high cost of the victory angered some of his officers and men. Morale remained high among the Urrea column even after Santa Anna's defeat at San Jacinto. The disastrous Centralist retreat from Texas (while some claimed that the campaign could still be won) caused morale to plummet.

Insurgents: Although many decried the unsettled civil and military situation, the insurgents remained firm in the belief in their superior fighting abilities. The defiance exhibited by the Béxar garrison in refusing to surrender or withdraw proved contagious. The executions conducted by the Centralists horrified and reinforced the determination among the insurgents to fight. The cries "Remember the Alamo" and "Remember La Bahía" proved to be very effective tools in creating the desire to achieve victory over the Centralists.

Endnotes

NOTES TO CHAPTER ONE

[1]Jack Jackson, ed., *Texas by Terán: The Diary Kept by General Manuel de Mier y Terán on His 1828 Inspection of Texas* (Austin: University of Texas Press), 100.

[2]For a modern study of Spain's loss of its New World colonies, see Robert Harvey, *Liberators: Latin America's Struggle for Independence* (Woodstock & New York: Overlook Press, 2000).

[3]For a review of Mexico on the verge of revolution, see Robert Ryal Miller, *Mexico: A History* (Norman: University of Oklahoma Press, 1985), 163-94.

[4]Ibid., 195-202.

[5]For two studies of Mexico's attempt to establish a republic after Iturbide's overthrow, see Stanley C. Green, *The Mexican Republic: The First Decade, 1823-1832* (Pittsburgh: University of Pittsburgh Press, 1987) and Timothy E. Anna, *Forging Mexico, 1821-1835* (Lincoln and London: University of Nebraska Press, 1998).

[6]For a study of the rise of Centralism, see Michael P. Costeloe, *The Central Republic in Mexico, 1835-1846: Hombres de Bien in the Age of Santa Anna* (Cambridge: Cambridge University Press, 1993).

[7]For an overview of Texas under Spain, see Donald E. Chipman, *Spanish Texas, 1519-1821* (Austin: University of Texas Press, 1992).

[8]For a study of Tejano society, see Andrés Tijerina, *Tejanos & Texas Under the Mexican Flag, 1821-1836* (College Station: Texas A & M University Press, 1994).

NOTES TO CHAPTER TWO

[1]Amelia Williams and Eugene C. Barker, eds., *Writings of Sam Houston* (5 vols.; Austin: University of Texas Press, 1938), 1:309

[2]David G. Chandler, ed. *The Military Maxims of Napoleon* (New York: Da Capo Press, 1995), 30. The literature on Napoleon and his effect on warfare is extensive. The following works were useful for this study: Christopher Duffy, *The Military Experience in the Age of*

Reason (London: Routledge & Kegan Paul Ltd., 1987); Gunther E. Rothenberg, *The Art of Warfare in the Age of Napoleon* (Bloomington: Indiana University Press, 1978); Brent Nosworthy, *With Musket, Cannon, and Sword: Battle Tactics of Napoleon and His Enemies* (New York: Sarpedon, 1996). The works of French military writers were translated and made available to waiting audiences in both the United States and Mexico. According to historical scholar David G. Chandler, a Spanish edition of Napoleon's *Maxims* appeared in Madrid as early as 1821. Proof of Napoleon's influence on the Mexican military can be found in the publication of a translation of Marshall Soult's work by a colonel of the Zacatecan militia, Manuel A. Cañedo, *Prontuario De Puestos Militares O Tratado De Fortifcacion De Campaña* (Mexico: Imprenta de la federacion en palacio, 1825).

[3]The effects of terrain on the Texas Revolution are discussed in James W. Pohl and Stephen L. Hardin, "The Military History of the Texas Revolution: An Overview," *Southwest Historical Quarterly* (January 1986); 269-308.

[4]John A. Lynn, *Bayonets of the Republic* (Champaign: University of Illinois Press, 1984), 64, 100; Alexis de Tocqueville, *Democracy in America* (2 vols.; New York: Vintage Books, 1945), 2:286-87, 295-96.

[5]The rivalry between regulars and volunteers is a theme developed in Richard Bruce Winders, *Mr. Polk's Army: The American Military Establishment in the Mexican War* (College Station: Texas A & M University Press, 1997).

[6]*Register of Debates*, House of Representatives, 21st Congress, 1st Session, 583.

[7]See Thomas W. Cutrer, *Ben McCulloch and the Frontier Military Tradition* (Chapel Hill: University of North Carolina Press).

[8]The classic study of the Spanish military in Mexico is Christon I. Archer, *The Army in Bourbon Mexico, 1760-1810* (Albuquerque: University of New Mexico Press, 1977).

[9]Joseph Hefter et al., eds., *The Mexican Soldier* (Mexico: Nieto-Brown-Hefter, 1958), 55.

[10]Ibid., 58.

[11]Although more modern studies of Santa Anna have been written, the classic remains Wilfrid Hardy Callcott, *Santa Anna: The Story of the Enigma Who Was Once Mexico* (Norman: University of Oklahoma, 1936).

[12]Robert V. Remini, the author of a multi-volume biography of Andrew Jackson has emerged as the modern authority on Old Hickory and his role in early American history. For a single volume overview of Jackson's life, see Remini's *The Life of Andrew Jackson* (New York: Penguin Group, Inc., 1990).

[13]The classic study of Sam Houston remains Marquis James, *The Raven: A Biography of Sam Houston* (Indianapolis: Bobbs-Merrill Company, 1929).

NOTES TO CHAPTER THREE

[1]John H. Jenkins, ed., *Papers of the Texas* Revolution (10 vols.; Austin: Presidial Press, 1973), 1:379. Hereafter referred to as *PTR*.

[2]For an in-depth look at the history of Coahuila y Tejas, see Vito Alessio Robles, *Coahuila y Texas, Dese la consumación de la Independencia hasta el Tratado de Paz de Guadalupe Hidalgo* (2 vols.; México: Editorial Porrúa, 1979).

[3]*PTR.*, 1:385.

[4]Ibid., 1:198-99

[5]Ibid., 2:31.

[6]Ibid.

[7]Stephen F. Austin, "General Austin's Order Book for the Campaign of 1835," *Quarterly of the Texas State Historical Association* (July 1907), 9-11. Hereafter referred to as "Austin's Order Book."

[8]Eugene C. Barker, ed., *The Austin Papers* (3 vols.; Washington, D.C. and Austin: American Historical Association and University of Texas, 1924-1927), 3:183.

[9]Ibid., 3:16-17.

[10]Ibid., 3:22-23.

[11]Ibid., 3:31.

[12]George Dedrick, "New Light on the Tampico Expedition," *Texas Historical Association* (October 1907), 1157-61.

[13]"Austin's Order Book," 50.

[14]*PTR*, 3:490-95.

[15]Ibid., 3:492.

[16]Ibid., 3:156-58.

[17]*General Regulations of the Army; Or, Military Institutes* (Philadelphia: M. Cary and Sons, 1821), 140-41.

Notes to Chapter Four

[1]David G. Chandler, *The Military Maxims of Napoleon* (New York: Da Capo Press, 1995), 74.

[2]*Journals of the Consultation* (Houston: Published By Order of Congress), 14-18, in H.P.N. Gammel, comp., *The Laws of Texas, 1822-1897* (10 vols.; Austin: Gammel Book Company, 1898), 1:518-22. Hereafter referred to as Gammel's *Laws of Texas*.

[3]Ibid., 39-40 in Gammel's *Laws of Texas*, 1:543-44.

[4]Two early studies provide valuable insight into the workings of Texas's revolutionary government: W. Roy Smith, "The Quarrel Between Governor Smith and the Council of the Provisional Government of the Republic," *Quarterly of the Texas State Historical Association* (April 1902), 269-345; Ralph W. Steen, "Analysis of the Work of the General Council, Provisional Government of Texas, 1835-1836," *Southwestern Historical Quarterly* (April 1937), 309-33; "Part Two: Analysis of the Work of the General Council, Provisional Government of Texas, 1835-1836," *Southwestern Historical Quarterly* (January 1938), 225-40; "Part Three: Analysis of the Work of the General Council, Provisional Government of Texas, 1835-1836," *Southwestern Historical Quarterly* (April 1938), 324-48. Also see Paul D. Lack, *The Texas Revolutionary Experience: A Political and Social History, 1835-1836* (College Station: Texas A & M University Press, 1992).

[5]*Journals of the Consultation*, 29, in Gammel's *Laws of Texas*, 1:533.

[6]Ibid., 33, in Gammel's *Laws of Texas*, 1:537.

[7]Ibid., 29, in Gammel's *Laws of Texas*, 1:533.

[8]Williams and Barker, eds., *Writings of Sam Houston* (8 vols.; Austin: University of Texas Press, 1938-1943), 5:366-67.

[9]Ibid., 1:305-306.

[10]Ibid., 1:308-309.

[11]Ibid., 1:309.

[12]Ibid., 1:311.

[13]Ibid., 1:312-13.

[14]Ibid., 1:314-15.

[15]*Proceedings of the General Council*, 30-31, in Gammel's *Laws of Texas*, 1:578-79.

[16]Ibid., 52-53, in Gammel's *Laws of Texas*, 1:600-601.

[17]Ibid., 83-84, in Gammel's *Laws of Texas*, 1:631-32.

[18]John H. Jenkins, ed., *Papers of the Texas Revolution* (10 vols.; Austin: Presidial Press, 1973), 1:371-73, 482-84, 3:61-64. Hereafter referred to as *PTR*.

[19]Ibid., 3:91-93.

[20]Ibid., 3:129.

[21]Ibid., 3:127-28.

[22]*Proceedings of the General Council*, 147-48, in Gammel's *Laws of Texas*, 1:695-96.

[23]*PRT*, 3:239.

[24]Williams and Barker, eds., *Writings of Sam Houston*, 1:321-23.

[25]*PTR*, 3:188.

[26]Ibid., 3:325.

[27]Ibid., 3:412-13.

[28]Ibid.

[29]Ibid., 3:438-41.

NOTES TO CHAPTER FIVE

[1]John H. Jenkins, ed., *Papers of the Texas Revolution* (10 vols.; Austin: Presidial Press, 1973), 4:237. Hereafter referred to as *PTR*.

[2]Ibid., 3:490-95. For a written and visual overview of the Alamo, see George Nelson, *The Alamo: An Illustrated History* (San Antonio: Aldine Books, 1998).

[3]Jesús F. de la Teja and John Wheat, "Béxar: Profile of a Tejano Community, 1820-1832," *Southwestern Historical Quarterly* (July 1985), 8-13; Andrés Tijerina, *Tejanos & Texas Under the Mexican*

Flag, 1821-1836 (College Station: Texas A & M University Press, 1994), 25-45.

[4]Vito Alessio Robles, *Coahuila y Texas, Dese la consumación de la Independencia hasta el Tratado de Paz de Guadalupe Hidalgo* (2 vols.; México: Editorial Porrúa, 1979), 1:327-35.

[5]Jack Jackson, ed., and John Wheat, trans., *Texas by Terán: The Diary Kept by General Manuel de Mier y Terán on His 1828 Inspection or Texas* (Austin: University of Texas Press, 2000), 16-18.

[6]Williams and Barker, eds., *Writings of Sam Houston* (8 vols.; Austin: University of Texas Press, 1938-1943), 1:319-20.

[7]*PTR*, 3:272.

[8]Ibid., 3:34.

[9]Ibid., 3:278-79.

[10]Williams and Barker, eds., *Writings of Sam Houston*, 1:325

[11]*PTR*, 3:424-25.

[12]Williams and Barker, eds., *Writings of Sam Houston*, 1:332.

[13]Ibid., 1:334.

[14]*PTR*, 3:458.

[15]Ibid., 3:472-73.

[16]Ibid., 3:499.

[17]Ibid., 505-506.

[18]Ibid., 4:15-16.

[19]Ibid., 4:14.

[20]Williams and Barker, eds., *Writings of Sam Houston*, 1:345.

[21]Ibid., 1:339-40.

[22]*PTR*, 4:123-24.

[23]Ibid., 4:127.

[24]Ibid., 4:174-75.

[25]Ibid., 4:176-77.

[26]Ibid., 4:185.

[27]Ibid., 4:237-38.

[28]Ibid., 4:159, 263-65.

[29]Ibid., 4:58-61.

[30]Ibid., 4:303.

[31]Ibid., 4:352-53.

[32]Ibid., 4:159.

³³Ibid., 153-55.

³⁴Ibid., 4:41, 160

³⁵Williams and Barker, eds., *Writing of Sam Houston,* 1:309.

³⁶Ibid., 3:268.

³⁷Ibid., 4:325.

³⁸Ibid., 4:303.

³⁹Ibid., 4:504-505.

⁴⁰Ibid., 4:303.

⁴¹Ibid., 4:51, 237-38, 317-18, 327-28.

⁴²Thomas Ricks Lindley, *Alamo Traces: New Evidence and New Conclusions* (New York: Republic of Press Texas, 2003), 323.

⁴³*PTR,* 4:320-21, 327-38.

⁴⁴Ibid., 4:339; Lindley, *Alamo Traces,* 309-10. Lindley contends that Neill, who was in Gonzales on Februray 13, 1836, appeared in Béxar the following day to personally settle the dispute between Travis and Bowie. Neither Travis nor Baugh mention Neill's return in their letters to Governor Smith.

NOTES TO CHAPTER SIX

¹Carlos E. Castañeda, ed., *The Mexican Side of the Texan Revolution* (Washington, D.C.: Documentary Publications, 1971), 12-13.

²John H. Jenkins, ed., *Papers of the Texas Revolution* (10 vols.; Austin: Presidial Press, 1973), 4:165-66. Hereafter referred to as *PTR.*

³Ibid., 4:350-51.

⁴Ibid., 4:423.

⁵Alan Huffines, *The Blood of Noble Men* (Austin: Eakin Press, 1999), 103.

⁶*PTR,* 4:443-44.

⁷Ibid., 4:456.

⁸Thomas Ricks Lindley, *Alamo Traces: New Evidence and New Conclusions* (New York: Republic of Press Texas, 2003), 83-171. Lindley believes he has uncovered evidence that additional reinforcements arrived some time after the Gonzalez Ranging Company. He advances the theory that David Crockett actually left the Alamo to guide a relief column to San Antonio.

[9]David G. Chandler, ed. *The Military Maxims of Napoleon* (New York: Da Capo Press, 1995), 60, 76-77.

[10]Santa Anna's order for the attack reflected the military doctrine of his day, as expressed in Appendix C: E. Hoyt, *Practical Instructions of Military Officers: CHAPTER XII - Of the attack of redoubts, field-forts, villages, and other detached posts,* (Greenfield, MA: John Denio, 1811), 296-301. Also see, Manuel A. Cañedo, *Prontuario De Puestos Militares O Tratado De Fortifcacion De Campaña* (Mexico: Imprenta de la federacion en palacio, 1825).

[11]*PTR*, 4:518-19.

[12]A good source for the report of both Crockett and Bonham can be found in Mary Austin Holley, *Texas* (Lexington, KY: J. Clarke & Co., 1836; facsimile edition, Austin: Texas State Historical Association, 1990), 354.

[13]Castañeda, ed., *Mexican Side of the Texan Revolution,* 7.

NOTES TO APPENDICES

[1]John H. Jenkins, ed., *Papers of the Texas* Revolution (10 vols.; Austin: Presidial Press, 1973), 2:23.

[2]*Telegraph and Texas Register,* March 12, 1836.

[3]Trevor N. Dupuy, *The Evolution of Weapons and Warfare* (New York: De Capo Press, Inc., 1984), 323-24.

Note on Sources

The Battle of the Alamo presents a challenge for any writer who takes it on as a subject. Most historical events are documented by a variety of sources. In the case of the Alamo, however, reliable sources are scarce. Our knowledge of the fate of the Béxar garrison comes from William B. Travis' letters and the memories of those who survived the battle. Mexican accounts present a compound problem: (1) they are in a language with which many writers on this side of the border are unfamiliar, (2) Mexican repositories are *terra incognito* to most writers, and (3) a definite bias exists against Mexican documents. Thus, writers have based their interpretation of the famous battle on relatively few sources.

The battle's status as a cultural icon also presents a challenge to writers. Some have been unwilling to question the "facts" surrounding the event. Writing, however, is an intellectual process that calls for inquiry. Others have made it a point to be iconoclasts whose aim is to smash the traditional interpretation, taking pleasure at upsetting those who cherish the legends associated with Alamo defenders. Although they may not realize it, both are engaged in a struggle for the cultural meaning of the Alamo. I have attempted to sidestep this debate by concentrating on developing the broader picture of the Texas Revolution as the context for the battle.

Alamo writers often find themselves involved in sometimes rancorous debates with other others. The root of these disputes is similar to the one that divided the Texas military. Who is best suited to write about the Alamo—professional or lay historians? Both seem to have an innate distrust of the other, something that makes a productive discourse difficult. The resulting clashes often absorb the attention of writers whose efforts would be better spent on research rather than defending the ground one they have staked out for themselves.

The following is a brief bibliography for readers who wish to learn more about the Texas Revolution and the Alamo. It is not intended to be a definitive bibliographic study but rather a supplement to the sources already cited within the body of this work.

Published Primary Sources

Asbury, Samuel E., ed. "The Private Journal of Juan Nepomuceno Almonte, February 1-April 16, 1836." *Southwestern Historical Journal* (July 1945), 10-32.

Austin, Stephen F. "General Austin's Order Book for the Campaign of 1835," *Quarterly of the Texas State Historical Association* (July 1907), 3-55.

Austin, William T. "Account of the Campaign of the 1835 by William T. Austin, Aid to Stephen F. Austin & Gen. Ed. Burleson." *Texana.* (Winter 1966), 287-322.

Barker, Eugene C., ed. *The Austin Papers.* 3 vols.; Washington, D.C. and Austin: American Historical Association and University of Texas, 1924-1927.

Chariton, Wallace O., ed. *100 Days in Texas: The Alamo Letters.* Plano, TX: Wordware Publishing, 1990.

Gray, William F. *Dairy of Colonel W. F. Gray: From Virginia to Texas, 1835-'36.* Houston: Fletcher Young Publishing Co., 1965.

Hansen, Todd. *The Alamo Reader: A Study in History.* Mechanicsburg, PA: Stackpole Books, 2003.

Jenkins, John H., ed. *Papers of the Texas Revolution.* 10 vols.; Austin: Presidial Press, 1973.

Journals of the Consultation in H.P.N. Gammel, comp., *The Laws of Texas, 1822*-10 vols.; Austin: Gammel Book Company, 1898, 1:506-48.

Proceedings of the General Council in H.P.N. Gammel, comp., *The Laws of Texas,* 10 vols.; Austin: Gammel Book Company, 1898, 1:549-636.

Williams, Amelia and Eugene C. Barker, eds. *Writings of Sam Houston.* 8 vols.; Austin: University of Texas Press, 1938-1943.

CAMPAIGN MEMOIRS

Castañeda, Carlos E., ed., *The Mexican Side of the Texan Revolution* Washington, D.C.: Documentary Publications, 1971.

Filisola, Don Vicente. *Memoirs for the History of the War in Texas.* 2 vols.; Austin: Eakin Press, 1987.

Peña, José Enrique de la, *With Santa Anna in Texas: A Personal Narrative of the Revolution.* Edited by James E. Crisp. College Station: Texas A & M Press, 1997.

CAMPAIGN STUDIES

Barr, Alwyn. *Texas in Revolt: The Battle for San Antonio, 1835.* Austin: University of Texas Press, 1990.

Hardin, Stephen L. *Texian Iliad: A Military History of the Texas Revolution.* Austin: University of Texas Press, 1994.

Huffines, Alan C. *Blood of Noble Men: The Alamo Siege & Battle, An Illustrated Chronology.* Illustrated by Gary Zaboly. Austin: Eakin Press, 1999.

Lord, Walter. *A Time to Stand: The Epic of the Alamo.* New York: Harper & Row, 1961.

Nofi, Albert A. *The Alamo and the Texas War for Independence, September 30, 1835-April 21, 1836.* Conshohocken, PA: Combined Books, 1992.

Potter, R.M. *The Fall of the Alamo.* San Antonio: Printed by the Herald Steam Press, 1860.

Santo, Richard G. *Santa Anna's Campaign Against Texas, 1835-1836.* Waco: Texian Press, 1968.

Tolbert, Frank X. *The Day of San Jacinto.* New York: McGraw Hill Book Company, 1959.

Winders, Richard Bruce. *Crisis in the Southwest: The United States, Mexico, and the Struggle over Texas.* Wilmington: Scholarly Resources, Inc., 2002.

Index